THE LAW OF ATTRACTION:
Making it Work for *You!*

Deborah Morrison & Arvind Singh

Manor House

Library and Archives Canada Cataloging in Publication

Morrison, Deborah
The law of attraction : making it work for you! / Deborah Morrison &
Arvind Singh.

Includes bibliographical references.
ISBN 978-1-897453-11-7

1. Self-actualization (Psychology). 2. Success--Psychological aspects.
I. Singh, Arvind, 1970- II. Title.

BF637.S4M674 2009   158.1
C2009-904981-3

Manor House gratefully acknowledges the financial support of the Government of Canada through the Book Publishing Industry Development Program (BPIDP), Dept. of Canadian Heritage, for our publishing activities.

To you the reader,
May you prosper in all ways.

Acknowledgements

We are sincerely grateful to our cherished family and friends who are truly inspiring.

We also extend sincere thanks to the following highly respected authors: Dr. Bernie Siegel, Dr. Joe Vitale, Dr. Michael Mirdad, and Scott Shaw.

We gratefully acknowledge editor Michael B Davie and Manor House Publishing for bringing our book on a wonderful journey of manifestation from dream to reality.

FOREWORD

By **Bernie Siegel**, MD

The Law of attraction: Making it Work for You! is a wise and informative coach, which can help you to attract what you desire into your life and guide you to true prosperity.

While reflecting upon what people would want to attract into their lives I recalled a moment when I was visiting with my 90+ year old mother-in-law. She was sitting in a wheel chair and dealing with many health problems. I wanted to give her an opportunity to vent her feelings and discuss her needs and so I asked her: 'What can I pray for, for you?' I want you all to stop and think about what your response to my question would be.

I was expecting my mother-in-law to ask me to pray that we attract a nurse into her room on a more regular basis to see to her needs, including providing clean underwear and overall extensive nursing care. Instead she shifted into a state of peace and said: 'World peace.'   In all the years I have been asking that question of thousands of people, less than ten have transcended their needs and answered as she did. However, think what the world and our lives would be like if we each sought to attract world peace.

We need to understand that we can attract prosperity, peace and more. They are all a part of the same process. And hope is real while false hope is an oxymoron, which doesn't exist. I am not talking about wishful thinking or false expectations and neither are the authors of this book. If you buy a lottery ticket you *could* win but it's a modest risk/expenditure – you won't gamble away your life savings buying a single ticket. I am talking about you becoming a responsible participant and not a victim or submissive sufferer on the journey through life.

Many are afraid to attempt to attract what they desire fearing that if it doesn't happen they have failed again and once more the guilt, shame and blame issue arises related to what they did wrong. Some may even feel that God is punishing them. Those unhealthy messages come from a variety of authorities in your life who gave you hypnotic messages and mottoes to fail and die by and not mottoes to be happy and live by.

This book will teach you about what mottoes you can live and thrive by and help you to realize your potential. 'What am I capable of?' *That* is the question you need to ask yourself, *not* 'what did I do wrong?' As Ruth Gordon says in the movie Harold and Maude, 'Reach out, take a chance, get hurt even, play as well as you can. Give me an L, give me an I, give me a V, give me an E; LIVE, otherwise you've got nothing to talk about in the locker room.' We are talking about behaviour patterns that are similar to what I see in survivors and not about statistics or about how fast or easy it is to do something.

What are you capable of? What is your potential? As Carl Jung said, 'The future is unconsciously prepared long in advance and, therefore, can be guessed by clairvoyants.' But I still look both ways before I cross the street. What we can learn is how to eliminate what is destroying our lives. And we can save our lives by attracting into them that which is life-enhancing and life-saving.

We can learn also that difficulties are a part of life but they can be utilized to our benefit. For example, if we use our pain, as we use hunger, to seek nourishment and a solution to our needs, we can redirect our lives and find what we need to sustain ourselves. Then, such pain can turn into a blessing.

We need to know that when we are a success, in terms of accumulating things, we are not happy but when we attract happiness into our lives we are a success. Prosperity is not just about material things. It is about being grateful for life. I had a young man in my office tell me that his father ruined his life when he was twenty-one. I asked what his father did and he answered, 'He gave me a million dollars so I had to be a success.' That is a sad story. What if he had used the money in a charitable way to create a better world; would he have been seen as a failure by his father? One of our children gave away his inheritance to fund the college education of a friend he met in Nepal. He taught me a lot about what we attract into our lives.

Next question: What would you say if you won the lottery and what would you say if you learned you had cancer? Since ninety-five percent of lottery winners, in one study, said winning ruined their lives, I think you should say, 'Oh God why me?' and if you develop cancer, 'What can I do with it?' When you attract those attitudes into your life many things can turn into blessings because of what they teach you about life. But be careful what you wish for.

Let me relate an illustrative story: Three men found a buried treasure worth a fortune. That night two of them went out to get dinner while one stayed in their hotel room to guard the treasure. When they returned from dinner they gave their friend a meal they brought back for him. He had decided to keep the treasure and so he shot them before eating the dinner they brought. The dinner was poisoned because the other two didn't want to share the treasure with him. When the cleaning woman surmised what had happened, she disposed of the treasure to prevent it from causing any further problems. No one benefited from the treasure that had caused so much harm. So be careful what you seek to attract into your life.

How do you start to attract what will help you to find peace and true prosperity? The first thing to do is to define who your Lord is. Find your higher power and if it is material things you will attract trouble into your life. It is no accident that Monday morning we have more suicides, strokes, heart attacks and illnesses. When you find the higher power that helps you to develop meaningful connections, express compassion and become creative you will find your life to be prosperous and rewarding.

When you find meaning in your life and inner peace your body benefits too. Your feelings create your internal chemistry. We are all like multiple personalities in a trance state for the majority of our lives but we can decide what that state is and what personality we display. When you fear life and relationships you are on a self-destructive path, living in a negative trance state. When you feel a sense of self-love and esteem you and your life and health will benefit and prosper.

To have this change happen and to attract what you need, you and your mind must become like still water. Then you can truly reflect upon your life and who you are and find a sense of meaning, which will attract what you desire. If you grew up with parents who gave you negative hypnotic messages when you were a child, now is the time when you can re-parent yourself and be born again.

Our state of consciousness is non-local. It affects us and the people around us. So again, even when we are not consciously aware of the effect we have upon others, by our thoughts and what attracts us we are creating an effect. As quantum physicists will tell you, 'desire and intention alter the physical world causing things to occur, which would not normally occur if they were not desired.' I personally like to add the word 'determination,' because I believe your passion to attract the things you desire makes things happen.

When you are having a hard time, do not blame yourself or feel you deserve to be punished. When you lose your car keys you are more likely to look for them than to feel God wants you to walk home. So when you lose your health or prosperity, go and look for it. You are not being punished you have simply lost something that you and others can help you to find again.

I found the various religious views shared in this book to be very meaningful and one line from the Talmud says it well, 'He who rejoices in the afflictions, which are brought upon the self, brings salvation to the world.' Think about Helen Keller or Mother Teresa and what they attracted into their lives. It is about healing your life and attracting peace, relationships and creativity. It is *not* about fighting a battle against your troubles – for when you do that, you empower your enemy.

This book can be a significant factor in your journey forward and work like a life coach – because when you bring together information and inspiration you attract what you desire and need. Your job is to rehearse and practice the message that you get from The Law of Attraction. A coach cannot change you unless you are willing to listen to the advice presented and show up for practice.

If life were perfect it would not be creation and mankind would be going nuts in a few weeks. We are not ready for perfection and we won't be until we all realize what we truly need to attract into our lives so that we heal our individual lives. Because, when we each heal our lives and prosper we will notice that the world is healed too as a by-product. That's how to bring world peace into being. You take responsibility for what you attract into your life and not by being responsible for the world but taking responsibility for what you attract into the world.

In closing let me say that much of this does not happen at a conscious level. I work with people's dreams and drawings because the unconscious speaks through symbols and often what we think we want or think is best for us is shown by the symbols to not be the best choice. That can relate to treatment for a disease, or a job you are thinking about or where to live.

Life is fascinating and mysterious. The most significant thing you can attract into your life is nothing. Why do I say this? It's because of the significance of the number 10 in our lives. The Zero and the One speak of creation. Life and creation come from the indescribable and so we call it nothing. Then the One is created but it still has nothing to compare itself with or relate to, and so you can multiply or divide one by one and you still have one. Life begins when 1+1 occurs and we have two.

When we are joined with our higher power, creation begins. When plants and animals are added we have three and four. And when you add 1+2+3+4 we have 10 again. No coincidence.

So, my friends; attract into your lives what will help us create a better world for the family of man and all living things. And remember, nothing makes everyone happy, nothing solves all your problems and if you have everything, you need nothing. So now it should be clear what you need to attract into your life.

The way to be immortal is not related to material prosperity but about the prosperity of the love you attract through your life and actions.

Ernest Holmes, in The Law of Attraction chapter in his book *The Science of Mind,* sums it all up very well:

Thought can attract to us that which we first mentally embody, that which has become a part of our mental make-up, a part of our inner understanding. Every person is surrounded by a thought atmosphere. This mental atmosphere is the direct result of his conscious and unconscious thought, which, in its turn, becomes the direct reason for, and cause of, that which comes into his life. Through this power we are either attracting or repelling. Like attracts like and it is also true that we may become attracted to something which is greater than our previous experience, by first embodying the atmosphere of our desire.

- **Bernie Siegel,** MD, author, *Faith, Hope & Healing*
and *365 Prescriptions For The Soul*

Introduction

By **Scott Shaw**

The reality of human existence is that each of us wants something. Though we have been warned against this human trait by salient beings such as *The Buddha* who tells us, 'The cause of suffering is desire,' this has not halted the path of human cravings.

The question must then be asked, 'Is what we desire guided towards solely making ourselves happier and fulfilled, or is it guided towards the betterment of society and this world?'

In either case, we ultimately find that 'What is desire' is based upon 'What is desire,' meaning, no matter how holy we believe our desires to be, they are based in our own personal cravings and our personal perspective of reality – *they are based on what we want.*

This being stated, 'What we want is what we want.' So, how do we go about getting it? In this reality, this world where we find ourselves, there are exacting metaphysical methods to draw what we want towards us. In this book, this is exactly what the authors present to you – a method to get what you desire.

This is the book you've been waiting for – the one that clearly explains how to tap into the powerful benefits of The Law of Attraction and reap its awesome rewards.

It follows where prior bestselling books on The Law of Attraction left off – but with new added dimensions: This book establishes reasonable expectations of what you can anticipate receiving from The Law of Attraction if you take a realistic approach and marry action and persistence with positive thinking and visioning.

Prior books on The Law of Attraction are also praiseworthy but were subject to overly simplistic interpretations by some readers. This led to disappointment, disillusionment.

An unintended negative side-effect has resulted, in some cases, via an overly simplistic interpretation equating The Law of Attraction with the power of wishful thinking.

When wishes fail to come true in the absence of related and necessary action, there is a resulting sense of betrayal that is both unfounded and unfair for the practitioner as this shallow view denies a deeper understanding of the truth and the power of The Law of Attraction. This has also led in some cases to a corresponding negative viewpoint which blames the victims of financial hardship or even physical and emotional-mental suffering on a supposed unwillingness to think happy thoughts.

This simplistic interpretation taken to its most extreme, blames the victim for physical, mental, emotional or financial short-comings and can cause those holding this belief to turn their back on those less fortunate and become selfish and uncaring.

Of course, nothing – not even The Law of Attraction – can prevent bad things from happening to good people whether they practice positive thinking or not. Clearly a deeper understanding is needed – and it's now provided in *The Law of Attraction: Making it Work for You!*

Comparative religion explorations, spiritual teachings, interpretive offerings and insights into various belief systems are also integral parts of this deeply soulful book that establishes true wealth goes beyond the financial to embrace health and happiness – success on many different levels.

Yet, ***The Law of Attraction: Making it Work for You!*** is also easy to follow and engaging, marrying insight and knowledge with readily understood language and practical applications to allow even the greenest novice a real opportunity to gain an understanding of the Law of Attraction and benefit through the understanding and application of this natural law.

Not surprisingly, this book immediately met with an array of rave reviews from leaders in this field who read the pre-published manuscript and very much liked what they read.

Among the leading teachers to weigh in was Dr. Joe Vitale, author, ***The Attractor Factor*** and ***Zero Limits*** and contributor to ***The Secret.*** He had this to say: 'Outstanding! The most in-depth explanation of how to use the Law of Attraction to get practical results I've seen yet. Get this one!' I couldn't agree more.

The Law of Attraction is about more than attaining material wealth - it is a means to help achieve success in life at every level - including spiritual, emotional and also material.

The Law of Attraction: Making it Work for You! truly does have the answers and approaches you've been looking for – and in an easy-to-follow, insightful format.

Enjoy this journey into a deeper and more fulfilling understanding of The Law of Attraction. This is your guide to a more fulfilling life.

– **Scott Shaw**, author, ***Zen O'Clock: Time to Be*** and ***The Zen of Everything***

Table of Contents
With Chapter Summaries:

WHERE ARE WE GOING?

There are two primary aspects to *The Law of Attraction: Making it Work for You!* Firstly, the development of an expanded awareness of abundance including a more comprehensive, holistic understanding of prosperity and secondly, practical approaches on how to make the Law of Attraction work for you. Have you already read about how to manifest abundance in your life and yet still feel like you need to learn more about how to really make the Law of Attraction work for you? *The Law of Attraction: Making it Work for You!* offers a rich, engaging and insightful journey that unveils your capacity to transform your life and provides you with easy steps that create total transformation and abundance in your life.

COMPARATIVE SPIRITUAL PERSPECTIVES ON PROSPERITY

This chapter explores prosperity from nine major faith and spiritual perspectives. Each of these traditions has something to say about prosperity and through their understanding, you can learn how to integrate prosperity based on these traditions.

This chapter delves into the mystery of how to understand true prosperity. You may have tried to manifest abundance in your life, however what is true prosperity? Exploring the origins of the word prosperity and examining an all-encompassing definition of true prosperity, we find that development of character qualities is essential for wealth. You'll discover the importance of association with a Higher Power and activation of your inner Energy Centres for increased balance and alignment. In this chapter, you learn how to increase the flow of money, abundance and well being in your life.

Learn how symbols will help to attract what you want in your life. Investigate the symbolism of Five Elements and the Kabbalistic Tree of Life. Both of them allow for the expansion of the Law of Attraction beyond previous understanding. Learn why a broader system with Five Key Energy Centres can allow for the Law of Attraction to work for you. Symbols are all around and you can use them in your life to develop your full potential, attract what you want and empower your intentions.

Before you can create intentions on any level, you need to start with peace. Learn how to become centered through meditation, visualization exercises and breathing techniques. As you connect to the spiritual side of life you will also feel inspired, harmonious and directed in your life. Symbols such as Circles, Mandalas, and Labyrinth are explored along with how they help you become centered. A connection with Spirit, as expressed in symbols and in the archetypes of Self and Child, will help you to recognize your own Self-worth.

CHAPTER 6   155

THE AIR CENTRE: FORMATION OF YOUR CHARACTER

The formation of your character is dependent on your thoughts, since: *As you sow, so you reap*. What you believe determines your character, self-image and self-confidence. So changing your thoughts and beliefs are important, yet surface-level affirmations are limited in value. For real change, you need to develop a way to observe yourself. This comes through listening to your inner dialogue. This chapter presents a method for recognizing and changing your thought processes. Techniques to build intentions are presented along with symbols and archetypes that reinforce mental growth, flexibility, and activate the Air Centre.

CHAPTER 7   175
FIRE: THE HEART OF EVERYTHING

Your emotional world is expressed by the archetypes of Hero, Lover and Altruist, which respectively involve Self-Love, Love of Others and Universal Compassion. Learn about the Kabbalistic Theory of Reactivity, which explains how Reactivity is opposed to Responsibility in life. Growth at the Fire Centre involves *Self-Transcendence* where you connect to something bigger than you. You then can find meaning in your life as love and compassion grow in your heart. Even suffering and pain at the Fire centre is meaningful, for through them you give expression to the human spirit to rise above or courageously face difficulties. This shows that genuine empathy, compassion and courage are important to your growth.

At the Water Centre, the tension is between the archetype of the Warrior and the Animal. The Warrior represents the energy of the Will through which you try to direct and control life. But the Animal within expresses your primal energies based on instinctual urges and drives. These conscious forces of Will expressed by Warrior and subconscious Energies of the Animal when integrated create true power and balance in life. The energies from Water element offer willpower, virility and power by which you can succeed in manifesting your desires.

This is where manifestation occurs on the physical plane. You learn to bless all that is around you with your presence. Your foundation for security and stability in relationships, finances and health are created here. The intentions previously contemplated are now manifested on Earth and you learn how to expand awareness. You also learn the importance of nurturing well-being for self and others through the Mother archetype. This chapter provides practical steps to build financial abundance in detail, so that your dreams are nurtured with a secure financial foundation.

Thos chapter provides a summary of the main points of the book, plus a summary of our own four-point formula of Spirit, Believe, Activate, Receive.

Words of Wisdom...

Life is a field of infinite possibilities
– Deepak Chopra

The Universe likes speed. Don't delay. Don't second guess. Don't doubt. When the opportunity is there, when the impulse is there, when the intuitive nudge from within is there, act. That's your job, and that's all you have to do... If you turn it over to the Universe, you'll be surprised and dazzled by what is delivered to you. This is where magic and miracles happen.
- Dr. Joe Vitale

Chapter 1

Where Are We Going?

This book is written with the purpose to dispel the cloud of confusion that has accumulated around the subject of the Law of Attraction. Great wisdom has been provided about The Law of Attraction by both classical and contemporary authors and teachers. In *The Law of Attraction: Making it Work for You*, our conscious intent is to *expand* on the great insights provided thus far. With expanded insights and deepened understanding of the Law of Attraction, our hope is that many more of you will move toward experiencing the real results of increased abundance in your life and the expanded happiness which is truly your Divine inheritance.

Clearly we are excited to be accomplishing two very important objectives in writing this book. Firstly, we will explore a deeper understanding of prosperity by considering various aspects of true wealth including spiritual and interfaith perspectives. Later we will look at integrating *total well-being* through the *Five Energy Centres* of Spirit, Air, Fire, Water and Earth. As you journey through each energy centre and its corresponding Element, you will find practical tools that will enhance your direct experience of prosperity. These tools are yours to discover and use according to your own individual inclinations and inspirations. The tools are firstly creative use of symbols and secondly meditative activation of your five energy centres based on ancient Kabbalah teachings. As all lasting change begins within, the approach followed in this book is for inner transformation first and foremost.

As of yet, some people have been left disappointed with the Law of Attraction. Why is this so?

Unfortunately, after reading, researching, and attempting to put the Law of Attraction philosophy into practice in day-to-day life, thousands of people are yet to see any tangible results. Others have experienced partial, incomplete or transitory results with their attempts at manifesting increased abundance. This broad spectrum of results extends even further into vivid contrasts with some people receiving the great results they were anticipating, yet others, in reality experiencing severe setbacks.

As Scott Shaw has previously described the simplistic understanding of Law of Attraction philosophy has led to some unintended negative side-effects, including wishful thinking where merely thinking positive thoughts or feeling good is considered enough to gain materialistic advantage. Visualization without accompanying action and self-development lacks the strength by which to truly create lasting and fulfilling transformation in your life. Moreover, the simplistic understanding of the Law has led to uncaring attitudes where victims of suffering are blamed for their difficulties. Supposedly the hardships are the result of their failure to think happy thoughts or to feel good.

People have been blamed for their life challenges and in extreme cases, cherished friends and family have decided to turn away from them, believing them to be the creators of their own misfortune. This view expresses a narrow understanding of the Law of Attraction as strictly about material gain. In fact, the Law also encourages love, service and compassion. For those unable to sincerely give themselves to others, hollowness exists in their hearts, which no amount of money or things can ever fill. The Law of Attraction is an ethical system based on character development not a mechanical system that can be manipulated for self-gain. How you treat yourself and others is as important as what you think or feel. The Law responds to authenticity, not manipulation. Your character defines who you are more than surface-level contrived personality. The Law, synonymous with Spirit and Universe, knows the depth of your Being. So it matches the vibration of your character, giving you the exact experiences you need for your growth. Only through growth in personal qualities can you overcome any limitations in life. While thought and emotions are part of your growth, they are only a part. All the Elemental energy centres together create total transformation, which was missing in many previous approaches to the Law.

Those who have benefited by the Law of Attraction manifested abundance with a holistic approach, experienced a broad spectrum of physical, intellectual, emotional, social and spiritual prosperity and then have gone further to use a portion of their prosperity to assist others in their journey to success. While many approaches are labeled the Law of Attraction, the fruits are different. Some lead to greater harmony where you are truly transformed, others only provide a narrow focus on material gain.

What is the reason behind some of the turmoil and dissatisfaction that has at times resulted from sincere attempts to put the wisdom of the Law of Attraction into practice?

We have written *The Law of Attraction: Making it Work for You!* out of a strong concern for those of you who have not, as of yet, experienced life transformation and abundance. We have also written this book for those of you who are good at manifesting materially yet are not experiencing abundance in other aspects of your life. Our concern is that the Law of Attraction has been subject to too much interpretation and the wrong interpretation. The Law of Attraction wisdom presented so far by various teachers and authors has been excellent, yet at times misunderstood. *The Law of Attraction: Making it Work for You!* will focus on expanding and clarifying your understanding of how to put prosperity teachings into practice to create a more complete and holistic experience of abundance in your life. Manifesting involves a deeper, more expanded understanding of what prosperity is and a more complete insight into how to make the Law of Attraction work for you.

Eckhart Tolle makes this *expanded* perspective crystal clear as he teaches:

The moment manifests from the totality of all that is.

We suggest that you keep the above insight in your awareness as you journey throughout this book.

Previous Law of Attraction teachings have made an important contribution in enhancing understanding of how to create prosperity in your life. As we expand on these previous teachings, you will gain a holistic vision and clear insight about prosperity. With this more complete wisdom at your fingertips, we trust that many of you will be satisfied with not only your enhanced understanding of the Law of Attraction but more importantly begin to directly experience greater results in your day-to-day lives. Realistically, life challenges will also continue to provide opportunities for enhanced inner growth. Your holistic journey begins with Spirit, where joy, happiness and peace are found.

Where have Law of Attraction teachings taken you in the past? To clarify and create a more complete overview it is useful to be aware of where you have come from. What previous perspectives on prosperity have been provided thus far? Each of the following important, contemporary authors has provided some instructive wisdom to assist you on your journey into experiencing increased prosperity in your life. A synopsis of their teachings is of vital importance in understanding where you have been thus far with prosperity knowledge.

In *The Secret*, Rhonda Byrne has gathered a variety of contributors, many who incorporate Law of Attraction principles into their seminars and books. Rhonda Byrne's central premise that is highlighted in her book is based on a quote from *The Emerald Tablet* circa 3000 B.C., '*As above so below, as within, so without.*' The many contributors to *The Secret* each add interesting facets of insight in order to help you understand The

Law of Attraction. Rhonda Byrne gives the reader three simple, basic steps to put into practice:

Ask
Believe
Receive

Simply stated, with these three steps, and primarily working with your thought, your journey into manifesting abundance in your life begins.

Secondly, Esther and Jerry Hicks provide material, including the book ***Money, and the Law of Attraction*** that centre around three clear steps to take in order to experience greater prosperity in your life:

Ask
Answer (The universe re-arranges itself)
Receive (Bring yourself into alignment with what you
          are asking for, i.e. Create positive feelings in
          alignment with what you are asking for)

You will discover that Esther Hicks, who channels her information from the entity Abraham, works primarily with bringing your vibrational being and feelings into alignment with that which your are seeking to manifest.

Thirdly, author and spiritual teacher, Michael Mirdad, provides clear insight into how the Law of Attraction looks when it remains *spiritually* focused. Mirdad sees all things, including prosperity, as being in their highest vibration when they follow a natural descent from Spirit to matter. His formula for the Law of Attraction is as follows:

Inspiration (from Spirit)
Focus (the mind and desires)
Action & Manifestation (a natural outcome)

The formula above is elaborated on in the following excerpt from some of Mirdad's teachings related to prosperity and abundance:

The above formula sets the tone or priority by placing God first or 'Seeking first the Kingdom of Heaven so all else can be added.' We accomplish this by allowing Spirit to be the inspiration or source of our ideas for whatever we create, rather than creating from our egos. Next, we focus our mind, desire, and intention onto the object of our inspiration. Here is where we give our inspiration a direction to follow. This is like drawing a blueprint for a new home that would otherwise remain a mere idea. Lastly, before we see the manifestation of our inspiration and focus, like our home in its completed stage, we must allow an appropriate balance of passivity (resting, waiting and allowing) and assertiveness (action, doing and initiative). There is a time for each but the trick is knowing which one to do and at which given moment. Following a process for manifestation such as this allows not only the frequent manifestation of our daily needs but also provides a peace, certainty, and ease that is beyond the understanding and capability of our ego and its methods for manifestation. The Law of Attraction can be summarized as follows: Creating from Spirit attracts more Spirit; creating from ego attracts more ego.

Michael J. Losier, author of **The Law of Attraction: The Science of Attracting More of What You Want and Less of What You Don't**, has also contributed significantly to understanding the Law of Attraction. Michael J. Losier explains the dramatic and powerful steps that you can practice in your life:

Identify desire
Give desire attention (Desire Statements)
Allowing (Have no doubt)

Michael J. Losier highlights the importance of allowing and acceptance of working with what is rather than doubting.

Joe Vitale in his informative DVD ***Install and Transcend The Secret***, provides three clear and simple steps to assist you in putting the Law of Attraction into practice:

Divinity
Believe
Receive

Joe Vitale explains the importance of making a connection with the Divine as well as the process of clearing, letting go of your inner obstacles and blockages to prosperity in order to receive.

James Twyman, in his DVD ***The Moses Code***, teaches that your awareness of *oneness* and connectedness is of utmost importance in your journey of personal life transformation. He explains that the biblical quote '*I am That, I am*' reflects the wisdom that awareness of *oneness* is essential as you journey through life.

Beneath the Surface

Each of the above contemporary prosperity teachers/authors (and the many other classical/contemporary providers of prosperity wisdom) contributes significant wisdom to light the way in your life transformation journey. Your increased abundance and prosperity may begin with one of these teachers and you may indeed experience the fulfillment that you were seeking. A certain teacher may provide the exact *missing piece of the puzzle* for your life, which does in fact work for you, so that results readily manifest to your satisfaction. Each of the prosperity teachers has their own unique style with their own particular point of focus, within a set paradigmatic framework, a unique way of understanding prosperity principles. A certain perspective may speak to your heart and soul. In contrast some of you have honestly tried to put these teachings into practice and have yet to experience results in your life. What about those of you who still seek results?

Much of the past focus on prosperity and the Law of Attraction has been on positive thinking and feeling good, but didn't touch on some underlying issues. It is as if what we have received thus far with prosperity wisdom is only the *tip of the consciousness iceberg*. To use an analogy, envision an iceberg, with the tip visible on the surface of the water. Most of the iceberg, in fact a huge portion of the iceberg, remains submerged beneath the surface of the water. The tip of the iceberg is symbolic of the focus on positive thinking and maintaining good emotional feelings that have been generally highlighted in much of the prosperity wisdom thus far. This wisdom is useful and effective for some of you who are attempting to manifest greater prosperity and abundance in your life, if in fact this wisdom happens to be the missing piece of the puzzle that you need to incorporate into your life. However, most of the iceberg that exists beneath the surface of the water is invisible. It is this enormous, invisible, as yet undiscovered portion of the iceberg that we will focus on in *The Law of Attraction: Making it Work for You!* By learning about the submerged aspect of the iceberg, along with the visible aspect of the iceberg you then discover, and move toward a *total* understanding of the iceberg; in other words a greater clarity about *total transformation* and abundance. We suggest a complimentary, integral approach. This book focuses on exploring the submerged aspect of the iceberg in order to create a more expanded understanding of how to experience progressive life transformation. By doing so we will also explain and understand some of the underlying issues associated with your journey into greater prosperity.

Expansion

Our material is intended to enhance, not contradict or downplay the presently existing teachings about The Law of Attraction. By integrating previous teaching (the tip of the iceberg) along with our teachings in *The Law of Attraction: Making it Work for You!* (the submerged aspect of the iceberg) a more *total* understanding and more expanded vision of prosperity is possible. If you have not manifested the prosperity that you have desired, then this information is for you. We hope that with this *expanded* vision of prosperity you will move on in your life toward manifesting the greater success and abundance that exists as of yet as a dream within the depths of your heart. We wish you happiness and joy as you experience such overflowing abundance that you may share it with others along the way.

Ralph Marston reminds us of the great importance of inner development in your journey of life transformation:

Success isn't something that you just go out and get. If you chase it, it will elude you. Instead, you attract success to you by the person you become. If you want to attract powerful people, you must become powerful. If you want to attract creative people, you must become creative. No one will be attracted to you just because you want something. But when you yourself become impressive, then impressive people will rally around you and be only too willing for you to stand on their shoulders. The world is full of dreamers who talk big and have impressive plans. No one cares about your dreams unless you back them up with action, discipline and commitment. Actions speak infinitely louder than words. The greatest thing you can ever offer anyone is the person you've become. If you want the world to give you value and wealth, then you must become a valuable person. Your most valuable asset is your own personal development. Make yourself competent, attractive, committed, disciplined, and skilled. Become the person you need to be in order to have the life you want. Invest in your future by investing in yourself.

Many people find it very difficult to transform/expand their realities. It is essential to keep on developing your inner virtues and good qualities of character, along with deepening your view of life. This is essential if you want to move forward in life. You can expand your reality by becoming aware of what you believe in, what you think and perceive about the world along with what you want to attract. It is important to start learning about your ability to deepen your perception and understanding of yourself and the Law of Attraction in order to expand your reality. The greater you expand your understanding about what prosperity is and how to make the Law of Attraction work for you, the greater will be the results you enjoy. Expand your understanding and awareness to experience better results.

Learn about your ability to manifest abundance with the help of new understanding, tools and techniques that we provide for you. Build upon what you have learned about prosperity thus far, what you believe in; and grow in wisdom and knowledge, both theoretical and practical about the Law of Attraction. You will need to move on from that which you currently put your belief in (give away your power to) be it success, love, money, etc. Discover the courage to move beyond your present comfort zone. Remember if you want to experience personal life transformation you must do one thing – expand! Use the tools and techniques presented in this book according to your own comfort and personal inclinations. Also it is important to clarify your dreams and visions in order to transform your life, as well as expanding your understanding of what prosperity means.

The following wonderful quote by Eckhart Tolle is about *expanding* your consciousness and you may find it useful to keep in mind as you journey toward manifesting greater abundance in your life:

All the things that truly matter-
beauty, love, creativity, joy, inner peace-
arise from beyond the mind.

In our book we will provide you with tools and techniques to not only work with your conscious and subconscious mind, but also to go beyond your mind by tapping into the power of your *Five Energy Centres.*

Start With Inner Peace

Within the simple framework that we have provided in this book, are insights into expanding on the principle teachings and approaches that make up the substance of all known Law of

Attraction philosophies and practices. If you read this book with an open mind and with integral, holistic awareness it is possible to easily unravel the mysterious Elements behind the Law of Attraction; Elements necessary to understand and incorporate into practice, so that you too may experience increased success in manifesting abundance in your life.

What is of utmost importance in starting to practice the Law of Attraction more effectively? *Begin with inner peace!* Now ask yourself; am I truly experiencing inner peace right now? The direct experience of real inner peace includes that wonderful feeling of peace, optimism, acceptance and joy; no matter what life conditions/situations that you may find yourself in. True inner peace is not dependent on a certain set of conditions in order to manifest abundance in your life. True inner peace is free from the limits of situation, circumstance, having or not having in your life. Inner peace is real. Inner peace exists in the very centre of your being and is the essence of who you really are. *I am peace* is the true nature of human nature. To know this and experience this in everyday life is to know and live in alignment with who you really are.

The experience of inner peace brings along with it clarity of mind, compassion of the heart, and a connection with the deep and vast essence of the infinite ocean, your *Spirit*. This approach is being in touch with your *Self-Worth* and thereby tuned into your inherent intuitive wisdom. With inner peace you are tapping into a *Super Conscious* state of being, an uplifted consciousness, transcendent beyond egoism and beyond a self-absorbed mindset. Released and free of the limits of ego, selfishness and a troubled emotional state of being that feels as if you are in a tiny row boat, tossed about by the winds of life circumstances on a stormy sea. Rather than this fearful, troubled state of being, you can make an inner connection with your true Self, your ever-present centre of inner peace. A centre that is infinite, vast as an ocean and yet still, calm like a crystal clear waveless lake. Calm, still and powerful. Your inner *Source*: of eternal optimism, power, stillness and intuitive wisdom.

From this transcendent state of inner peace, you begin to embark on your journey of life transformation for the purpose of increased abundance and prosperity, not only for yourself alone, but for the good of all.

Interestingly, with inner peace, you will calmly work with the Law of Attraction, consciously setting your intention and manifesting greater abundance. Yet, you will remain just as calm, and peaceful with whatever the results may be, for you will know that the universe does in fact work in grand, and mysterious ways. Your hope and trust remains constant as your acceptance and gratitude for all that manifests along the way becomes ever more complete. In gain or in loss, your intention is set and remains steady in knowing that in all conditions *I am peace.* With inner peace you will also clearly know that your true point of power is always in the *now*, regardless of whatever life condition you found yourself in the past. From the life situation that you are in right now, your vibration of inner peace will launch you into an accelerated experience of manifesting greater peace and prosperity in your life. How do you experience inner peace? By simply setting your conscious intention to do so!

Throughout our book *The Law of Attraction: Making it Work for You!* we will expand further on ideas about inner peace in order for you to firmly establish a more solid foundation from which to generate an expanded understanding and experience of how to make prosperity manifest in your life. Inner peace is the true starting point for your Law of Attraction practice.

Mystery

There is always an element of mystery to life! Mystery is found in the current times within our contemporary society. We are in a *New Era.* The Earth has *shifted* beneath our feet! Interestingly, there is a *New Energy* that surrounds us. Traditional roles, systems, and solutions do not necessarily always work. Have you considered that what you are hoping to manifest may in fact be a solution to your situation based on the Old Energy that is no longer applicable? Therefore, you must remember that we do not always have the Universal perspective, and sometimes it is for the best not to receive in exact accordance with your request. Consider the recently released Walt Disney family movie called *The Secret of the Magic Gourd.* This movie portrays a young boy who receives absolutely everything he wishes for instantaneously as he wishes for it. There is consequence to this immediate gratification: Chaos and confusion, as well as the lack of character building that result from earning something without genuine effort. This is why the idea of a genie merely granting wishes stands opposed to character building. What you earn through developing solid qualities creates the solid foundation upon which to build your growth. We would like to remind you that there is always a dimension of mystery that remains while working with the Law of Attraction, since this mystery is an inherent aspect of life. How does the Universe work in mysterious ways?

Throughout **The Law of Attraction: Making it Work for You!** we remind you that we all *receive* filtered through Universal compassion and order. Therefore, we suggest that you keep an open mind as you put the Law of Attraction theory into practice.

Intuitive wisdom is also a great and mysterious inner power that you possess and can access. As you practice the Law of Attraction we suggest that you remain spontaneous, embrace the mysterious and potent flow of Universal energy in your life; be ready to make changes in some of your plans, listen to your higher guidance/inner voice of intuitive wisdom and integrate this knowledge into your life. But what if you are trying to incorporate all of these newfound prosperity insights and practical techniques into your life and you still feel that you are not manifesting results?

When all else fails, maintain a vibration of inner peace, go to the *Source* and then take some kind of compassionate, inspired action – get the energy moving throughout your entire being and in your life, even if this is only in a small way.

Get the energy flowing, moving and be open, creative and generous. Remember to never give up, for in giving up you stop the energetic flow of life force. Once again, remember that your point of power is in the *now*, right in your current situation. The *now!* Know that if you are unable to change a particular situation right this instant, you are always free to decide how you respond to the situation. Decide to respond with inner peace!

Balance

As William Wordsworth once said:

The best part of a man's life is his little, nameless, unremembered acts of kindness and love.

We suggest that you bring a balanced approach into your practice of the Law of Attraction. Ask yourself *who am I doing the Law of Attraction for?* From a highly spiritual perspective we are all one. From a sociological perspective we are all inter-dependent. As the well known saying goes *No man is an island, no man stands alone...* We are a truly inter-dependent humanity.

We are free and unbounded by circumstance to create greater prosperity and abundance in life, while also assisting to empower and forward one another. Therefore, remember to practice the Law of Attraction with the conscious intent to *balance love toward self with love toward others.*

Know that the *Law of Indirect Action*, which is all about creating good for others is a law that creates a highly energetic Universal energy flow that eventually comes back to you also; as increased abundance and prosperity in one form or another in life. Similarly, the *Pay it Forward* principle highlights the value and effectiveness of spontaneous action.

Be open to the other person, not closed, and be willing to assist for the greater good. A self-absorbed approach creates a decreased Universal energetic flow. In contrast, by *Paying it Forward* you experience an increased Universal energetic flow.

Journey to Higher Spiritual Ground

Be aware that your journey in life is not only about getting what you want or getting rid of what you don't want. You are here to grow both extrinsically and intrinsically. You are ultimately here to demonstrate virtues in life and to build character.

Know that it is sometimes through your greatest life challenges that the most wondrous display of virtues are developed and expressed. Therefore, accept your life experiences, even as challenging as they might be.

Know that some aspect of prosperity will manifest eventually even if you must live through a life challenge. Similarly, know that life will inevitably, at times, have its challenges. The Law of Attraction will never eradicate all challenges from life, for challenges are part of the inherent nature of life and ground for emotional as well as spiritual development. Rather, we would suggest that you embrace the challenge while attempting to put your more expanded understanding of prosperity into practice.

In this book, we intend to bring your understanding about prosperity to higher spiritual ground with holistic and spiritual expansion on understanding of true prosperity, as indicated through the analogy of the *iceberg* previously explained.

Also, we provide an expanded understanding of the *Five Energy Centres* and how they relate in a most important way to understanding the process of manifesting prosperity.

Balance is a highly important aspect in working with your *Five Energy Centres*, in order to create a balanced and open flow of Universal energy and prosperity in your life. We provide easy, practical tools and techniques for you to put into practice.

Along with the *Five Energy Centres* you will be given an integral, holistic understanding about the significance of working with the *five elements*. The *five elements* of Spirit, Air, Fire,

Water and Earth are important aspects to work with in expanding your understanding of prosperity and in moving toward a greater ability to experience the results that you seek.

Included in our understanding of how to receive increased results in attempting to experience life transformation are four components: *Spirit, Believe, Activate, Receive.* Thereby, you'll be able to increasingly take a quantum leap into the *New Energy*, an expanded experience of increased abundance. You'll discover the Law of Attraction at play in a more complete, holistic and integral manner in your day-to-day life.

We understand that the Law of Attraction needs to be balanced with your capacity for *love*, *empathy* and *compassion*, so that we avoid blaming victims of natural disasters, abuse, disability, poverty and disease for their life situation. How can a life without compassion be truly prosperous? If you don't care for others, then by the law of attraction, why should they care for you?

We emphasize that other people and their reality are important – you can practice the Law of Attraction *for both yourself and others*, with the intention of creating *a world that works for everyone!*

As the Dalai Lama teaches:

Right action is always compassion.

We must balance love for self with love for others. Realize that it is your time *now*. It is a moment in time *now:* for you to receive an opportunity for expanded understanding and experience of the Law of Attraction in order to more effectively make it work for you! We encourage you to take this journey into that deep, vast, infinite ocean that is your *Soul*. And so it begins, your journey of discovery and life transformation…

Consider the following quotes and prayer as your starting point of reflection:

God grant me the serenity
to accept the things I cannot change;
courage to change the things I can;
and the wisdom to know the difference.

Reinhold Neibuhr

Watch with glittering eyes
The whole world around you,
Because the greatest secrets
Are always hidden
In the most unlikely places
Those who don't believe in the magic
Will never find it.

Roald Dahl

Key Points

- Where have we been?

- Beneath the Surface

- Expansion

- Start with Inner Peace

- Mystery

- Balance

- Journey to Higher Spiritual Ground

Bibliography for Chapter 1

Byrne, Rhonda.   *The Secret.*

Beckwith, Michael.   *Spiritual Liberation: Fulfilling Your Soul's Potential.*

Canfield, Jack.   *The Success Principle.*

Dahl, Roald.   *The Best of Roald Dahl.*

Marston, Ralph.   *The Daily Motivator.*

Mirdad, Michael.   *The Seven Initiations of the Spiritual Path.*

Tolle, Eckhart.   *A New Earth.*

Twyman, James.   *The Moses Code.*

Vitale, Joe.   *The Key: The Missing Secret for Attracting Anything You Want.*

Chapter **2**

Comparative Spiritual Perspectives on Prosperity

INTRODUCTION

The previous chapter, highlighted the importance of *expanding* your understanding of *prosperity* and *the Law of Attraction* if you really want to *make it work for you.* This chapter explains that as you *expand your understanding* of prosperity you are, in a sense, creating a larger *foundation* for your abundance to manifest.

Making the Law of Attraction work requires a solid *foundation* of expanded understanding of abundance. *Expanded understanding* is an important *tool* necessary to build not only your *foundation* but also to *activate* other aspects of manifestation in your life. Conversely, a narrow understanding of the law of attraction leads to constrained, inconsistent or even non-existent results.

This chapter is inspired by a quote by the late Swami Vishnu Devananda, founder of numerous Sivananda Yoga centres, who said: 'The paths are many but the Truth is one.' We decided to explore various fascinating world religions and spiritual paths, and discover what they teach about manifesting prosperity in your life. Each religion's prosperity perspective is presented in one clear, concise statement. From these statements, one universal prosperity verse is created.

The following spiritual teachings offer insights on the manifestation of prosperity and the process of personal life transformation. Prosperity includes material wealth, yet it also includes balance with spiritual values. The following is a journey through nine of the world's major religions and what they reveal about true prosperity.

CHRISTIAN

What are some of the highlights of Christian teachings on prosperity and how to make it work for you in your own life? Does Christianity advocate and even romanticize poverty as a Christian ideal? Conversely does it encourage you to aspire toward creating a life inclusive of abundance?

Let's start with the Third Epistle of John. John is communicating with Gaius, who John wants to see prosper. John says:

Beloved, I pray that you may prosper in all things and be in health, just as your soul prospers (3 John 1:2)

In this verse two types of prosperity are highlighted: Firstly, spiritual and secondly material prosperity. Spiritual prosperity is indicated when John speaks 'just as your soul prospers,' while material prosperity is expressed by 'that you may prosper in all things and be in health.'

Matthew 6:19-21 contrasts spiritual and material prosperity:

Do not store up for yourselves treasures on earth, where moth and rust destroy, and where thieves break in and steal. But store up for yourselves treasures in heaven, where moth and rust do not destroy, and where thieves do not break in and steal. For where your treasure is, there your heart will be also.

Jesus is contrasting between 'treasures on earth,' ravaged by moth and rust, and 'treasures in heaven,' eternal and untouched by moth, rust and thieves. The treasures in heaven are virtuous qualities that remain eternal and untouched. Where you put your heart glorifies that particular treasure.

Emma Curtis Hopkins emphasizes the virtues of love as a Christian response to difficulties in life: *All people will change when you know that they are love. We shall change toward all people when we know that we ourselves are formed out of love. All is love. There is nothing in all the universe but love.*

Many Christian teachers encourage that obstacles in life be approached with the healing power of love, so that we resist not anything but allow love to transform reality.

St. Catherine of Siena, similarly, emphasizes spiritual prosperity: *If you are what you should be, you will set the whole world on fire.*

Also, reflecting the spiritual centre in Christian teachings of prosperity are the words of St. Francis of Assisi when he reminds us: *'If we endure patiently and with gladness, thinking on the sufferings of our blessed Lord, and bearing all for the love of Him: Herein is perfect joy.'* Virtuous qualities expressed by Christian teachers offer resolve and self-control necessary to manifest a full life of both spiritual and material abundance.

Christian teachings also indicate that you cannot serve both money and God, (Matthew 6:24). You need to be clear about your priorities in life. You start by being in harmony with God and then consider prospering materially.

Material prosperity is guided by compassion expressed through charity for those less fortunate. These values are present in the following prayer:

THE PRAYER OF SAINT FRANCIS OF ASSISI

Lord,
Make me an instrument of thy peace.
Where there is hatred let me sow love;
Where there is injury, pardon;
Where there is doubt, faith;
Where there is despair, hope;
Where there is darkness, light; and
Where there is sadness, joy.

O Divine Master,
Grant that I may not so much
Seek to be consoled as to console;
To be understood as to understand;
To be loved as to love.
For it is in giving that we receive,
It is in pardoning that we are pardoned, and
It is in dying that we are born to eternal Life.
- St. Francis of Assisi

With the emphasis on spiritual prosperity first Jesus advises: '*But seek first his kingdom and his righteousness, and all these things will be given to you as well*' (Matthew 6:34). To prosper in all things includes health, wealth, business and family life; in other words to manifest abundance in all aspects of your life. Therefore abundance is consistent with Christian values so long as it flows out of spiritual life. This is why The Lord's Prayer asks God to satisfy our daily needs not our greed: '*Give us this day our daily bread*' (Matthew 6:11).

Christian teachings also emphasize altruism with the instruction of Jesus to 'love your neighbour as yourself' (Mark 12:31). The Golden Rule of doing to others what you would have them do to you (Matthew 7:12). The altruism arises from the idea of reciprocity in action. In essence, what you do to someone else, you do to yourself. The Parable of the Good Samaritan (Luke 10: 25-37) extols the virtue of helping a stranger. The stranger is left beaten and robbed by the side of the road. A priest and a Levite both pass by without helping but a Samaritan stops:

A Samaritan, as he traveled, came where the man was; and when he saw him, he took pity on him. He went to him and bandaged his wounds, pouring on oil and wine. Then he put the man on his own donkey, took him to an inn and looked after him. The next day he took out two silver coins and gave them to the innkeeper. 'Look after him,' he said, 'and when I return, I will reimburse you for any extra expense you may have.

The Samaritan displayed compassion and being a good neighbour as he helped the Jewish man robbed and beaten. This parable is an ideal expression of compassion and service in Christianity, since it illustrates the importance of:

1. Showing compassion
2. Taking initiative to help
3. Bearing the cost when helping another

Christian theology highlights that material prosperity is good but it must not sacrifice faith. St. Paul in First Epistle to Timothy admonishes: *For the love of money is a root of all kinds of evil. Some people, in their eagerness to get rich, have wandered away from the faith and caused themselves a lot of pain.*

Christian theological wisdom clearly explains what is of paramount importance in relation to desire for abundance; while you may pray for material prosperity in effect your greatest need is spiritual prosperity that lasts forever. Ultimately as you concentrate on prospering spiritually it is God with Divine Wisdom and Grace that will bless you in all other ways.

Some modern Christians think that you need a lot of money to prove God's blessings. However, true prosperity in Christian teachings is spiritual gifts based on being blessed with virtuous character and conduct. Remember that God has a purpose for blessing you with a lot of money. In Luke 17, Jesus says: *The*

Kingdom of God is within you. Many times people seek riches outside when the real wealth is inside you – in your character qualities, and in who you become with Divine blessings.

CHRISTIAN QUOTES

Command those who are rich in this present world not to be arrogant nor to put their hope in wealth, which is so uncertain, but to put their hope in God, who richly provides us with everything for our enjoyment
– **St. Paul,** (1 Timothy 6:17-19)

Be on your guard against all kinds of greed; a man's life does not consist in the abundance of his possessions
– **Jesus,** (Luke 12:15)

Faith is to believe what you do not see; the reward of this faith is to see what you believe!
– **St. Augustine**

Father, forgive them, for they do not know what they are doing – **Jesus,** (Luke 23:34)

JEWISH

The three major Abrahamic religions are Judaism, Christianity and Islam, which recognize Abraham as a common patriarch. As Judaism is the oldest of the Abrahamic religions, its texts and traditions have exerted great influence on the others.

Early Judaism viewed wealth and good fortune as a sign of Divine blessings, while suffering as the result of moral failing. Therefore, early Jewish thought advocated that the suffering of *the righteous is not understandable.* Later writers of the Hebrew Bible, tried to understand this dilemma of why bad things happen to someone good as seen in the Book of Job.

Job is a man of virtuous character but Satan suspects that he only serves God because of his comforts. So God allows Satan to test Job and in one day he loses his livestock, servants, and children but he still maintains great integrity. Finally, Job is afflicted with sickness but he still holds his faith. He is confused why these awful things happened to him. His friends insist he must have sinned and must repent. All Job knows is that despite being righteous, he still suffers.

The Book of Job raises many questions about justice and suffering. Job points out the heartlessness of a doctrine where those suffering are blamed for their situation. The story of Job highlights these lessons on suffering:

1. The cause of suffering is at times unknown
2. Even with challenges continue to have confidence
3. Suffering is not always the result of personal failing
4. Avoid judgment and criticism of those suffering
5. Offer unconditional support to those in need of comfort

Even after all his sufferings, Job is practical and recognizes the value of money. When asked by God which he would prefer poverty or afflictions, Job responds that he would accept afflictions but not poverty, since without some money both he and his family would be wretched. Job's story also teaches the importance of dignity and self-worth. Even after all his losses, Job recognizes his self-worth and maintains self-confidence. So in the end, he is twice as wealthy as before his trials.

Prosperity requires that you bounce back and start again as Job did. So if you are struggling with money, take heart that so long as you have inner self-worth, you can reconnect to your wealth. Still material wealth is a temporary gift because you are only a steward of this wealth. Judaism considers money is good but on its own we cannot rely on it to bring happiness. So you need to know how to be a good steward of wealth, and how much is enough money to meet your own needs and those of your family.

In essence, Judaism teaches the pursuit of physical comforts as essential for happy and prosperous life, so long as you use them with wisdom. Since God is the creator of everything then humanity can offer praise of thankfulness to God for what has manifested in life.

Forgetfulness of God and forgetfulness of the responsibility to others can lead to great suffering, according to Jewish teachings. The *memory* of God and suffering convert the past into a new and creative present that leads to the manifestation of life. Jewish theology calls for active involvement in the world, including uplifting the poor and creating a more just world. Prosperity moves from a strictly personal realm to creating a better world for everyone and for future generations. Judaism asks you to take responsibility for the world, including creating prosperity for yourself, your family, and making the world more prosperous.

JEWISH QUOTES

That which is hateful to you, do not do to your fellow. That is the whole Torah. The rest is the explanation; go and learn
– **Rabbi Hillel the Elder**

Do not seek revenge or bear a grudge against one of your people, but love your neighbour as yourself. I am the LORD
(Leviticus 19:18)

It hath been told thee, O man, what is good, and what the LORD doth require of thee: Only to do justly, and to love mercy, and to walk humbly with thy God (Micah 6:8)

To everything there is a season, and a time to every purpose under heaven: A time to be born, and a time to die; a time to plant, and a time to uproot what is planted (Ecclesiastes 3:1-3)

A good name is more desirable than great wealth. Respect is better than silver or gold (Solomon 22:1)

ISLAMIC

Islam encourages success and balance in life through responsibility, devotion to God (Allah), and the correct use of knowledge. All three plant the seeds of prosperity in families and consequently for peace to flourish among all people on Earth.

Basic understanding in Islam is that spiritual belief and practice are interconnected. Islam accepts both the spiritual and physical needs of a person, since faith only has meaning when practiced in the world. Accordingly, a set of practices is integral to uplift character of a believer. Afterward prosperity is manifested on strong ethical principles.

The practice of daily prayers purifies the mind and heart, and increases virtues such as patience and discipline. Prayer creates devotion and a unity to a higher purpose in daily life. The discipline acquired through prayer can help in success in other areas of life, including learning to save, budget and wisely spend.

Donating to charity is based on purity of intention and it purifies your heart and income. Other advantages of giving include: Redistribution of wealth, reduction of suffering, removal of greed and selfishness, and creation of social responsibility.

Fasting during the daylight hours in the month of Ramadan allows a Muslim to develop devotion to God by prayer and thanksgiving before starting and breaking the fast each day and during the month. Dedication, willpower, patience and self-control are also developed. Most importantly, the temporary deprivation during the fast allows for greater understanding for the suffering of the hungry and poor.

Islam encourages the attainment of wealth and material progress through legal and moral channels. Nevertheless, material wealth is recognized as temporary because you leave it behind you upon death or setbacks that can separate you from it. The Quran instructs that you are merely a trustee of the wealth for a period, since the real owner is Allah (6:165). You can release grasping tendencies with money through contributing some of it to help others. In the process, selfishness, greed, oppression and injustice are avoided.

The Quran recommends practice of justice and honesty in all your transactions (55:9). With the strong insistence on justice and honesty, Islamic law discourages and can revoke any business deal that involves injustice, exploitation or cheating. Since Islam is considered a complete system of life, it is concerned with maintaining the rights of the individual in commerce, while ensuring high morality and ethics in business transactions.

Islamic teachings encourage sharing of wealth along with moderation in spending: *Give to your family their due rights, as also to the poor, and to the wanderer. But squander not your wealth in the manner of a spendthrift* (Quran 17:26).

While encouraging modesty in spending, the Quran asks to give freely to help others in need (3:134). As Islamic teachings advocate justice, donating your wealth is important as part of being a good caretaker of wealth. In order to do this development of empathy for those in need through fasting is essential.

Ali ibn Abi Talib says: *The worst poverty is poverty of the soul.* So when measuring poverty and wealth, we need to measure the transformation that occurs at psychological and spiritual levels. In essence, to have prosperity in life you take responsibility to transform your life and contribute to help others.

ISLAMIC QUOTES

Allah has revealed to me that you should adopt humility so that no one oppresses another.
- **Prophet Muhammad**, Riyadh-us-Salaheem, (Hadith # 1589)

Even as the fingers of the two hands are equal, so are human beings equal to one another. No one has any right – nor any preference to claim over another.
- **Final sermon of Prophet Muhammad**

Do not turn away a poor man...even if all you give is half a date.
- **Prophet Muhammad**, Al-Timidhi, (Hadith # 1376)

The best richness is the richness of the soul.
- **Prophet Mohammed**

Do not say about anything, "I am going to do that tomorrow," without adding, "If God wills' (Quran 18:23-24)

SIKH

The first is truthfulness, second honest earning and third charity in God's name. The fourth is pure intent of mind, and the fifth is the Lord's admiration and praise
– **Guru Nanak** (Guru Granth Sahib, pg. 141)

The five principles enunciated above by Guru Nanak highlight the golden path to prosperity in Sikhism. *Truthfulness* as the first principle means to recognize Oneness of God and humanity. All creation emerged from the One Source and so divisions of race, religion, caste, class and gender are social and economic divisions, not intrinsic to the order of the universe or to human nature. What then creates separation from the original oneness?

The Universe first manifested through the Divine Mother during periodic cycles of creation, stability and destruction (Guru Granth Sahib, pg. 7- line 2). As the universe expanded, multiple streams of creation arose with evolution of various creatures (Guru Granth Sahib, 3-17). This led to great diversity of life and consciousness differentiated from original state of Oneness through development of individuality and ego. A duality then emerged between self/others, Divine/human and object/subject relationships. Repairing this duality and recovering innate Oneness creates prosperity in all aspects of life, for when you connect to the Divine Ocean, you are no longer a tiny stream.

From Truthfulness emerges the second principle of *Honest Earning*. Material wealth is important for growth and success in life and pursuit of it is encouraged within ethical limits of honesty. If money is gained through exploitation, then at a spiritual level it is taking you away from the prosperity found in peace. As you need both peace and material wealth, how money is earned is as important as accumulating it to benefit both yourself and others.

Once you have earned enough for yourself and your family, then you have a responsibility to practice *Charity*. Sharing with others can involve your money, time or skills. Your time dedicated to help in your community through Service is highly regarded in Sikh practice.

Whatever action you perform whether with Earning a Living or Giving through Charity, you need *Pure Intent* behind it. Otherwise what you do will only add to your pride and boastfulness. Those vices can detract you from spiritual growth. Social life requires that you practice pure intention because then people trust that your thoughts, words and actions are aligned.

Praising the Lord is showing gratitude for your gifts and blessings. Whatever aids in your growth is considered a gift, even challenges. When you thank the Divine for all blessings, it shifts your awareness to the abundance that is already in your life. As you do so, your thought shifts from limited to infinite possibilities in your life.

Virtuous qualities are important for prosperity in Sikhism, since true prosperity rests with your character. Self-effort to develop good qualities is important but force is ineffectual in manifesting abundance. Only a natural state of spontaneity and effortlessness can return you to the original purity before creation and before your birth. Guru Nanak affirms that force in actions is useless, since it causes you to go against the current of your natural state as you respond only to surface anxieties, tensions and emotional triggers rather than connecting to your natural state called *sahaj*.

Sahaj is the effortless intuitive awareness based on serenity and abiding peace. When you are in *sahaj*, the ego naturally becomes silent. Ego arises from divided or dualistic mind where social and cultural conditioning creates a sense of separation from those around you. You forget the Giver of life, of breath, and all the gifts you enjoy in pursuit of ego-based goals. Yet underneath the ego, *sahaj* innately resides undisturbed as the natural presence of your true nature.

Sahaj literally means 'born together,' since it reunites you with who you are – the spontaneous expression of you underneath social conditioning.

As *sahaj* rises to the surface, illumination, heightened consciousness, intuitive knowledge and flowing activity become part of your life. With ego-based tensions subsiding, emotional integrity naturally emerges as tensions are loosened. Even pain and pleasure pass like surface ripples, while the depth of your being remains calm.

Peace and happiness experienced though *sahaj* are essential to prosperity in life. *Sahaj* requires no forced action because it effortlessly arises with wisdom. When service, devotion and prayer are sincere and spontaneous, they can lead to *sahaj*. Guru Nanak shows the life of people living in *sahaj* in this passage:

Those who abide in sahaj look alike on friend and foe. What they hear is essence true and in their seeing is meditation. They sleep in calm and rise in peace. From 'being' to 'becoming' with natural ease. Sad or glad, they abide in sahaj. Effortless their silence. Spontaneous their utterance. In poise they eat, in poise they love. In sahaj they find distances bridged (Guru Granth Sahib, 236-18/19).

Guru Amar Das writes that the spontaneous *sahaj* is even experienced through the sound-current of devotional music or sacred word as the mind gets absorbed (Guru Granth Sahib, 1234-7). For this reason, music and singing plays an important role in Sikh worship because the music and the message contained in the compositions offer release from conditioned ego-based thinking.

Through Divine Grace you can reconnect to your natural state and with virtuous qualities you can attract abundance. Here is a list of vices and the corresponding virtues to overcome them:

VICE	VIRTUE
1. Lust	1. Love
2. Anger	2. Forgiveness
3. Greed	3. Contentment
4. Delusion	4. Truth
5. Pride	5. Simplicity

Virtue rests on moving from self-centredness to altruism as you begin to understand that your prosperity is tied to the growth of others. Guru Arjan clarifies this in these words:

The God-conscious being looks upon all alike like the wind which blows equally upon the king and the beggar
(Guru Granth Sahib, 272-12/13).

Sikh teachings encourage ethical business practices, along with contributing to social welfare and social justice around you through donating your money and time.

Thus, living according to Five Sikh Principles of Truthfulness, Honest Earning, Charity, Pure Intent and Lord's Praise; and developing your Five Virtues are golden paths to manifest spiritual and material prosperity.

SIKH QUOTES

One who sees that Light within each and every heart understands the Essence of the Guru's Teachings
– **Guru Nanak** (Guru Granth Sahib, 20-8)

In that place where the lowly are cared for; there, the Blessings of Your Grace rain down
– **Guru Nanak** (Guru Granth Sahib, 15-8)

Make Good Deeds the Soil, and let the Sacred Word be the Seed; Irrigate it continually with the Water of Truth. Become such a Farmer and Faith will sprout
– **Guru Nanak** (Guru Granth Sahib, 24-1)

Your soul, breath of life, mind and body shall blossom forth in lush profusion; this is the true purpose of life
–**Guru Arjan Dev** (Guru Granth Sahib, 47-19)

Truth is higher than everything but higher still is truthful living
– **Guru Nanak Dev** (Guru Granth Sahib, 62-11)

HINDU

Hinduism is the oldest currently practiced religious tradition in the world. Hinduism is varied being derived from variety of texts and practices. It encompasses an expanse of practical human goals and lofty spiritual ideals. Even with great diversity, the Hindu faith has a common faith in a cosmic order called Dharma, meaning righteous, duty and law. It is the foremost gateway to manifesting abundance in your life. Hindu teachings explain that the practice of Dharma as cosmic universal law results in an experience of strength, tranquility, peace and joy within yourself and in your life. When aligned to your Dharma, to your duty, you act in any given situation so as to achieve righteousness.

So with Dharma the expectation is that everyone follows prescribed duties. These duties would include rituals, service to family, community, ancestors and God. Thereby, in order for a person to manifest prosperity both materially and spiritually one must live in harmony with the prescribed Hindu teachings on Dharma, as right action relevant for your age and position in society. The emphasis in Hinduism is on duty and less on individual rights, so prosperity is measured within the wider context of your responsibility to family, society and dharma.

The following quote from the sacred Hindu text The Bhagavad Gita reflects some further insight on right action:

O son of Prtha, that understanding by which one knows what ought to be done and what ought not to be done, what is to be feared and what is not to be feared, what is binding and what is liberating, is in the mode of goodness.

Dharma is the foundation of all human pursuits in life traditionally based on your birth and stage in life. In the modern context, Dharma can relate to your duty based on age, family, society, career and spiritual life. In the Hindu stages of life, your first quarter of life is as a Student where you learn Dharma from a teacher who helps you to form good values.

As you consider other human pursuits, you hold on to Dharma as the foundation of your ethical and moral principles.

The second quarter of life as a Householder is devoted to pursuit of Material Wealth called *Artha*. Here you selflessly carry out your duties to family and society, fulfilling your civic duties and work in profitable labour. The main goal is to acquire material wealth, achieve widespread fame, and an elevated social status.

Along with *Artha*, as a Householder you also pursue *Kama*, which includes sensual gratification, sexual fulfillment, desire, and artistic enjoyment. You delight in the pursuit of pleasures and devote your energies to achieve your desires.

At the third phase of life as a Retired person you start to realize that pursuit of Material and Sensual goals is partially satisfying. So you start to question life and develop a spiritual orientation.

With the fourth phase of life in Hindu ideals of the Four Stages of Life, you become a Renunciate, giving up on material and sensual pursuits. You focus on *Moksha* or liberation of Self from earthly bondage and to transition from life.

While the cosmic law is contained in Dharma, your own actions also produce a law called *karma*. Your actions produce cause and effect of good and bad actions with consequences, which are revealed in this lifetime or determine your next birth through reincarnation.

Karma always produces sweet and bitter fruits according to what you plant.

You can overcome Karma by separating from the fruits as you are dedicated to duty or love of a deity, family or to your society with selfless devotion.

In terms of Law of Attraction, the importance of what you plant and later harvest is integral to the manifestation process. Once you realize that what you do produces consequences, then you can take responsibility and correct the flow of your actions.

HINDU QUOTES

Whosoever offers to Me with devotion a leaf, a flower, a fruit, or water – that offering of love, of the pure of heart, I accept
– **Krishna** (Bhagavad Gita 9:26)

To action alone hast thou a right and never at all to its fruits; let not the fruits of action be thy motive; neither let there be in thee any attachment to inaction
 – **Krishna** (Bhagavad Gita 2:47)

May that be ours for which our prayers rise, may we be masters of many treasures! (Rig Veda 10.121.10)

Prosperity is not for the envious, nor is greatness for men of impure conduct
– **Saint Tiru Valluvar** (Tirukkural)

Find and follow the good path and be ruled by compassion. For if the various ways are examined, compassion will prove the means to liberation
– **Saint Tiru Valluvar** (Tirukkural)

BUDDHIST

In the teachings of the Buddha good qualities such as generosity, wisdom, patience, truthfulness, determination, compassion and mental stability are emphasized for prosperity and growth. Buddhists are asked to take full responsibility for their body, speech and mind. The most important is the intention behind them. The Buddha makes this clear in this quote:

All mental states have mind as their forerunner, mind is their chief, and they are mind-made. If you speak or act with an impure mind, then suffering follows you just as the wheel follows the hoof of an ox
–Buddha (Dhammapada, verse 1)

All your intentions whether positive or negative create seeds in your mind. These seeds are the *karma* that you acquire from your desires. The Buddha taught that everything that happens has a specific cause or set of causes. For example in order to become sick you must come into contact with germs and one must be weak enough for the effect of 'sickness' to manifest. Thus, Buddhism teaches that everything that happens does so because of a cause or set of causes, which produce *karma*.

Buddhist ethics take a psychological perspective and avoid specific prohibitions or laws, and instead certain teachings offer training for the mind, body and speech. Central to Buddhism is the interdependence of all sentient beings, which carries a moral responsibility for you to consider the good of others. Accordingly, compassion governs Buddhist ethics for prosperity. Happiness and abundance result from caring for one another. In order to develop good qualities and prosperous life, Buddhism includes ethics, meditation and practices for the development of wisdom. Through wisdom you develop an accurate understanding of the world. With mental stability, compassion, joy and peace increase, leading to balanced and prosperous life.

Another important condition for a prosperous life is Right Livelihood by which you earn according to teachings of not harming, not taking what is not given, and not to make false statements. As a middle way between extremes of self-denial and self-gratification, Buddhism supports the acquisition of food, clothing, shelter and other essentials, so that your anxiety over them is eliminated. On the other hand, the teachings caution against excessive attachment to money. Money itself is neutral but the attachment to it can create an imbalance. A prosperous life let's you enjoy money and keep it in perspective.

The Buddha taught the importance of developing your heart and mind in manifesting a prosperous life. When you accept scarcity mentality either as lack of material wealth or compassion, then you fail to seek what is best for everyone. Prosperity starts with thinking abundant and generous thoughts.

BUDDHIST QUOTES

If you want others to be happy, practice compassion. If you want to be happy, practice compassion
– Dalai Lama.

Whether one believes in a religion or not and whether one believes in rebirth or not, there isn't anyone who doesn't appreciate kindness and compassion
– Dalai Lama

Thousands of candles can be lighted from a single candle, and the life of the candle will not be shortened. Happiness never decreases by being shared
– Buddha

Have compassion for all beings, rich and poor alike; each has their suffering. Some suffer too much, others too little
– Buddha.

I cannot have pleasure while another grieves and I have power to help him
– Buddha (Jatakamala)

SUFI (Islamic Mysticism)

Sufi teachings advocate that initiation, initiative, free will, and conviction are linked to prosperity in life. Initiation and initiative are derived from *initial* meaning a beginning. So when you take initiative or undergo an initiation you are beginning a new phase. Initiatives can be material, cultural, religious, or spiritual in nature. To *take initiative* emerges from free will. Although reasoning can hold you back from taking initiative it is your reasoning power that helps you to accomplish your purpose.

Every *initiative* taken by great creative souls has been powerful since there was conviction and faith as to its outcome. Therefore conviction is of paramount importance when *taking initiative* to manifest prosperity in your life. *Initiative* can be taken without any logical explanation, such as when inspired by knowledge and also when an initiative is thought about through spiritual understanding bestowed upon a person as the heart is open to the *silent call* or the intuitive *inner voice* of Higher Guidance.

In order to manifest prosperity Sufi belief advocates that you must pass tests of life. These are life tests where you must display qualities such as humility, patience, faith, truthfulness and sincerity. Sufi teachings regard *initiation* as most sacred.

In relation to prosperity one basic Sufi principle is of paramount importance that being *sincerity in humility*. *Happiness* is considered to be an unfolding of the inner self and comes as an expansion of consciousness. The deeper the spiritual realization of a person, the more humble he/she becomes.

Finally, the Sufi understanding of *true prosperity* is to realize *true happiness.* Sufi wisdom teaches that Greatness is in *humility; wisdom is in modesty, success is in sacrifice and truth is in silence.* Sufi prosperity is shown with the following approaches to life; to live simply, do our work, do all we can, do it thoroughly, do it whole-heartedly, and do it quietly.

Greed for a hundred worldly glories is beggary;
When you reach contentment poverty is wealth
- Indian Sufi poet Bedil

Is it desirable for every soul to take initiation/initiative? The word initiation means *to go forward* and the Sufi perspective is that progress is life and therefore it is always advisable to try to go forward in business, professions, political life and spiritual advancement. However, the most important Sufi lesson on prosperity is *patience*; we must begin all things with patience.

SUFI QUOTES

When the mind is focused and tranquil, the intuition becomes more active. One hears a deep, still small voice from within, the intelligence of the heart, which guides one to happiness and prosperity through spirit and understanding
– James Dillehay

Sufis believe that, expressed in one way, humanity is evolving towards a certain destiny. We are all taking part in that evolution
– Idries Shah (The Sufis)

You are only living when you are graced in the moment by the moment
– Adnan Sarhan.

Let the beauty of what you love be what you do
– Rumi.

Love demands from each a mystic silence
– Farid al-Din Attar.

WICCA/PAGAN

Wiccan prosperity teachings focus on working with various forms of two important techniques: Firstly, to envision and secondly to focus on your desires. The Wiccan belief is that your thoughts create your experience. As a result by using the power of your mind to envision and focus you are able to manifest abundance in your life. For the most part Wiccan thought does not advocate that a symbol will necessarily result in creating what that symbol represented in the physical realm. With envisioning, focusing, casting a spell/circle, or obtaining a charm what is of primary importance is that through these techniques you can create a more balanced state of mind; and with a more balanced state of mind you have more power from within to use in working toward creating more of what you want in life.

You can create your own techniques to work with your thoughts in order to manifest abundance. One Wiccan approach to prosperity is to obtain some *charms* as symbols of what you may want to attract in your life. For example, charms as symbols for true love, good fortune, wealth, safe travel etc. Dedication may be used in order to activate a charm that is symbolic of what you want to manifest in your life, and then place the charm in your home, pocket, and bag or on a key ring. Remember that miracles can happen and wishes can come true.

Spell Casting is a commonly recommended Wiccan practice that assists you to manifest your prosperity in life. You can create your own spell, composed of elements that symbolize or represent your heart's desire. The main point is to create a symbol for what it is that you desire to manifest: To envision and focus your desires on your intended result by means of creating a symbol or series of symbolic steps to assist in manifesting your heart's desire. Prosperity will be yours.

Another approach to manifest your desires is as follows: Before a ritual, or casting a spell or circle, evoke the energies of the four quarters in a focused way (North, South, East, West). By doing so this gives you increased power to bend matter to your choosing. By aligning with the energies of the four quarters you can create *magic.* Wiccan traditions assign specific colours to represent the four directions, known as the four quarters. For example, North, the element of Earth, can be represented by a green candle, and is used to evoke knowledge and to receive deeper wisdom. Thus, *magic* involving prosperity, wisdom, patience and truth are appropriate for use with a green candle.

Most importantly, remember that Wicca is an ancient practice and Spell-Casting must always seek the good of all. Also remember that before physically drawing out a spell or a circle the importance and power is that state of mind that casting the circle puts you in. Your state of mind is of utmost importance, and rituals can help you process and control your mind.

Wicca affirms that *you* are the power and by balancing your state of mind you are able to invoke that power with charms, or by casting a spell or circle. By means of seeking to control and balance the forces/power within you it makes transformational living possible; in order to live wisely and well without causing harm to others, also to live in harmony with nature, and to manifest prosperity and abundance in your life.

WICCAN QUOTES

I have all that I need and I live within my means, whatever I do not have is on its way to me
– **Philan.**

Through the Goddess, we can discover our strength, enlighten our minds, own our bodies, and celebrate our emotions
– **Starhawk.**

Magic is not always serious or solemn. It is a joyous celebration and merging with the life-force
– **Scott Cunningham.**

KABBALAH (JEWISH MYSTICISM)

Kabbalah is about humanity and a *general desire to receive*. In effect, G-d created you with this desire. This *will to receive* includes all creatures. According to Kabbalistic teachings at the end of *restoration* everyone will know G-d, from the youngest to the eldest. The restoration is a process of exchanging intentions from egoistic ones to altruistic ones. This means from merely benefiting oneself to benefiting the Creator and the entire creation.

Kabbalah means *original wisdom* and can transform your life along with the entire world; in fact it is believed that the world can be transformed into paradise on Earth and eventually manifest Heaven on Earth. To do this practical tools are offered in order to effect authentic change in your life; and thereby create order out of chaos. Some of these tools are meditation, fortification of consciousness, developing a strong and positive state of mind, to never give or receive jealous glances or looks or ill will, and transcending the ego.

Kabbalah teaches that the purpose of Creation is to obtain communion with the Creator, since only in communion with the Creator can humanity achieve fulfillment, happiness and lasting peace. Each division of this *will to receive* is called a soul. It is believed that with the correction of each soul, the entire world ascends into true spirituality; spirituality meaning ongoing communion with the Divine and thus spirituality being understood as true prosperity.

Kabbalah asserts that you are here on this Earth because you asked to be here, and as Yehuda Berg teaches: *so that you could experience what it means to be a creator...instead of having endless paradise handed to you freely by your Creator, you desired something far better: the chance to have a hand in actually creating that endless paradise. In short, you wanted to become a proactive participant in the process of creation rather than remain a reactive bystander.*

Finally, Kabbalah teaches that in order to achieve prosperity in life tell yourself: *I am never a victim; I am responsible for everything that happens in my life - And for understanding that it happens for the best.*

KABBALAH QUOTES

To fulfill its giving nature, the infinite force of energy created a receiver- in Kabbalah it's called a Vessel
– **Yehuda Berg**

It is well known to researchers of nature that one cannot perform even the slightest movement without motivation, meaning without somehow benefiting oneself
– **Yehuda Ashlag**

The Creator wants to fill us with the very best. And until a man receives all the very perfect and the very best that has been ordained for him by the Creator, he experiences the lack of everything, and this is the sign that he hasn't yet reached the goal of the creation
– **Baruch Ashlag**

Our spiritual task is to stop resisting the giving nature of Energy and let our Vessels fill up and runneth over
– **Gail Hudson**

CONCLUSION: After a thorough perusal of various religious insights and spiritual paths on prosperity that we have researched, one can only conclude that in essence the inter-faith, universal vision of prosperity/abundance consists of relationship: conscious relationship with oneself, others, the Divine/Infinite Spirit, and the entire Creation. A compassionate spirit of oneness approached with an open heart and mind is of paramount importance in achieving an expanded awareness and understanding of prosperity from a spiritually universal perspective. Finally, as a personal creative exercise in the prosperity and manifestation process, we took some time to reflect deeply on each of the nine religious prosperity teachings that we have researched. We then proceeded to condense each religion's central teaching on prosperity into one clear statement. As a humble gift to you (the reader) we have compiled each of these religious prosperity insights into 'One Universal Prosperity Verse' in hopes that with reading this verse your heart and mind will open with compassion, insight and inspiration into an expanded spiritual, universal understanding of prosperity (manifest from comparative spiritual perspectives). Conjointly this is the message that various religions share with us about life transformation, prosperity and abundance.

ONE UNIVERSAL PROSPERITY VERSE

MANIFEST FROM COMPARATIVE SPIRITUAL PERSPECTIVES

Bring memory of the Divine and of human suffering into the moment (Jewish)

Live in harmony with principles of Truth and Love (Christian)

Adopt humility and help one another (Islam)

Live with truthfulness, Honest Earning, Charity, Pure Intent, and Praise of the Divine (Sikh)

The practice of Right Action results in Strength, Peace, Joy within and in your life (Hindu)

Good qualities such as Wisdom, Generosity and Compassion bring true prosperity (Buddhism)

Live with patience, sincerity and humility (Sufi)

Envision and focus on your desires (Wiccan)

Live with altruistic intention and be open to all possibilities (Kabbalah)

Bibliography for Chapter 2

Berg, Yehuda — *The Red String Book: The Power of Protection*

Dominguez, Dr. — Jewish Beliefs,' May, 2006.

Jinger, Jarrett — 'Understanding Prosperity Christianity: Are Christians supposed to Be Rich,' 2007

Kahaner, Larry — *Values, Prosperity and the Talmud*

Lawton and Morgan — *Ethical Issues in Six Religious Traditions*

New Orleans Mistic — 'Green Spells Index: Wiccan Prosperity,' Spell 2007

Perez Ana, Mushida Rabia — 'Christi Initiation,' 2006

Ponder, Catherine — *The Prospering Power of Love*

Shirazi, Ayatollah Sayyid Murtada — 'The Teachings of Islam: Some Strategic Policies to Combat Poverty'

Sufi Movement International — U.S.A. Initiation

Chapter 3

UNDERSTANDING TRUE PROSPERITY

The Law of Attraction can help you achieve true prosperity, but here it is important to understand what true prosperity really is and to know that it encompasses much more than financial wealth. It is also important to realize that bad things can still happen to good people who think positive thoughts.

An unfortunate side effect of prior Law of Attraction books is that they were interpreted by some readers in a very superficial way to assume that you always get what you wish for. This resulted in a selfish mindset and a tendency to blame the ill and destitute for their woes. This chapter goes to the heart of what true prosperity and positive thinking is really all about.

WHAT IS TRUE PROSPERITY?

To further understand 'true prosperity' it is helpful to look at the origin of the words. 'Prosperity' surfaced in the English language c.1140, derived from the Latin word 'prosperitatem' which means 'good fortune.'

'Wealth' surfaced in the English language c.1250 and means 'happiness' and also 'prosperity in abundance of possessions or riches' and is derived from Middle English 'wele' meaning 'well-being' and 'wealthy' as a synonym for 'rich' is recorded from c.1430

'Well-being' can be further understood by considering firstly the meaning of 'well' derived from Old English 'wel' meaning 'in a satisfactory manner' and the Old English 'Willan' 'to wish.'

'Be' is derived from the Proto-Indo-European base 'bheu' and 'bhu' meaning 'to grow, come into being, become.' And from Sanskrit 'bhavah' which means 'becoming' and 'bhavati' becomes, happens and 'bhumi' earth, world are also derivations.

Thus the 'well-being' derivation shows meaning equivalent to 'wish or will better existence' or 'to become better.' Finally, 'wealth/wellness' can be better understood as meaning 'to act to make well' or 'the quality or state of being well.'

Therefore, by considering the etymology or origin of the words 'prosperity' and 'wealth' we learn that these words are originally derived from words such as 'good fortune,' 'well-being' and 'wellness.'

The original meaning of 'well-being' is 'to wish or will a better existence' and 'wellness,' as 'to act to make well.' Thus, prosperity and wealth both, according to the original derivation of the words mean 'to wish or will a better existence' and 'to act to make well.'

To gain a more comprehensive understanding of prosperity let us consider some insights. As Gerry D. Smith in his article 'What is true prosperity' reminds us, when you live your life by the Law of Attraction, you can create all you need. True prosperity starts within the mind and means more than just money, although money is also an aspect of true wealth.

Character qualities such as compassion, ideas, dreams, wishes and thoughts are all important parts of your prosperity consciousness. So whenever you focus your attention on a specific idea, wish or dream, it can become real.

Nevertheless, how you tap into your inner power, inner energy centres, Higher Power, and how you develop and express character qualities will affect how, if and when your desired intent will manifest.

By means of activating your five inner energy centres and the inherent power of your mind you can often attract whatever you focus on. Once you really know this with all of your heart, mind, body and soul, and with every cell of your being then amazing results will manifest in your life.

Doubt, fear, egoism, lust, anger, greed, hatred and jealousy are all thoughts and emotions that are counter-productive to understanding and expressing true, holistic prosperity. If there is enough faith behind your intent or request then there is enough power from within you to make it happen. Furthermore, know too that your natural awareness and association with a Higher Power is the true source of your prosperity. Thus, your spiritual belief is an important part of this source.

We invite you to know your Higher Power in an authentically personal way; that Higher Power can be understood from varying perspectives such as Inner Energy Centres, or the Divine Power that is omniscient, omnipresent and omnipotent. So activate your Higher Power according to your own understanding and what is most comfortable to you.

Interestingly, Yehuda Berg in his book *True Prosperity: How to Have Everything* explains that true prosperity is composed of many elements and may include some of the following sources: Physical, intellectual, emotional, social and spiritual well being. Some examples of true prosperity are good health; healthy eating and living; fulfilling relationships with family, spouse, friends, neighbours, co-workers and associates; a sense of belonging in community; a rewarding career along with sustained mental and emotional growth; and, satisfactory and worthy material possessions and financial wealth. *All* these are important ingredients for creating and maintaining true wealth.

Note that during times when you are feeling happier you can create your own destiny with greater ease. Similarly, negative moods can lead to the creation of negative events.

Although moods can vary from time to time, the more you focus on creating good moods the more positive experiences will manifest for you. Thus, thought and emotion are primary aspects that influence the process of the Law of Attraction and the creation of wealth in your daily life.

Still, you can be thankful for negative moods if they do occasionally occur since they serve as a 'contrast experience' and as markers for learning experiences that teach you how to consciously know what it is you do not want in your life.

Therefore, it is wise not to worry about or resist negative moods but rather relax, breathe deeply, process through them and learn something valuable from them that enhances your awareness and enables you to practice the Law of Attraction with greater wisdom.

True prosperity is composed of many elements and your thoughts and emotions significantly affect the progress of the Law of Attraction as in the case of money. When you give, you get back much more.

When you give cheerfully and with kindness prosperity will find you. A challenging experience can shape your character, so it is important to learn from mistakes. This involves the development of virtues and strong character qualities.

You can always attract prosperity by thinking, feeling, speaking and acting in positive ways. Have you ever noticed that your relationship with money gets *restricted* when you don't give it with a cheerful, loving attitude?

Consider that emergencies such as household items, dental, children's needs, and car repairs, etc. can suddenly create extra expense when you least need it. You meeting your financial responsibilities are important. As you give, let go of any guilt, self-pity or ill wishes toward others. As your wisdom and character grows, abundance flows with ever-increased synchronicity. True prosperity won't happen if you hold onto resentment, revenge, or fear. Therefore, replace negative feelings with positive ones and have an open mind to receive outcomes that are extraordinary. With this attitude you can create more outcomes that are positive and thereby practice the Law of Attraction in effective ways in order to understand, see and experience true prosperity in your daily life. Remember, as character and wisdom grows, abundance flows.

THIS IS NOT TRUE PROSPERITY: A CONTRAST EXPERIENCE

Three friends had together decided to learn more about creating increased prosperity in their lives, and their names were John, David and Sam.

They discussed together about what they had learned in relation to the Law of Attraction. Together they agreed that thoughts create your reality, so they decided to practice positive thinking in order to manifest greater abundance in their lives.

John very soon came across a key contact to increase his business investments and within a few years became a very wealthy man. David, however, even in face of his best efforts developed terminal cancer and soon was facing his last year of life. Sam made a carefully considered career move, however a few years later was faced with downsizing and therefore unemployment.

When John heard about the health and career challenges that were facing his two friends he said: 'You made your choices,' and he stopped associating with them out of fear that their negative vibrations would disturb his fortunes. He blamed their life challenges on their negative thinking and foolish choices.

David blamed Sam for making a foolish career choice and Sam accused David of negative thinking and repressed anger that caused his cancer. Both David and Sam criticized John for being selfish and greedy.

Thus a lifetime friendship dissolved within a few years after these three friends studied Law of Attraction insights. Once some varied results of success or life challenge surfaced along the way, they began to cast blame on each other, unable to enjoy their friendship and assist to ease suffering as friends. They became poor from the perspective of the losing their friendship.

This is a clear example of a 'contrast experience' and this is not the correct practice of the Law of Attraction. True prosperity also includes compassion and hope even in the face of difficulties. True prosperity includes quality relationships offering support through life's challenges and also sharing in the joy of success.

A beautiful, quality life-long friendship dissolved abrasively after learning about the Law of Attraction teachings and mistakenly attempting to put them into practice in a superficial manner.

METAPHYSICS OF TRUE PROSPERITY

A metaphysical understanding of true prosperity is to be in touch with your 'inner wisdom' of your Higher Self. An example of this would be experiencing a moment of penetrating insight; and in that moment you fully understand that your true nature is beyond any boundaries. This state of super-charge or *Superconsciousness* is openness to all the messages, both conscious and subconscious. Ultimately true prosperity is realizing your inner potential – the power of your thought and using it to create the life you want.

The metaphysics of prosperity teaches that you do create your own reality. Metaphysical understanding on prosperity reveals the nature of reality; that the order of the universe is the consistency of the Law of Attraction, and that you have free will. Metaphysically the Law of Attraction is a law that is so consistent and precise that everything that vibrates in harmony with everything else comes together.

Most importantly, those who understand this Law and get it 'balanced' will absolutely thrive in the sense that their inner worlds and outer worlds are better aligned! The metaphysics of prosperity and the Law of Attraction simply states that 'like attracts like.'

EVERYTHING IMAGINABLE VIBRATES

Everything imaginable vibrates, including your thoughts and attracts that which matches it under any and all conditions. The Law of Attraction is the organizing force and designer of your 'outer world.' This Law is what directs the electron. It is what makes the choice between all possible events.

The way things come together and move apart under the Law is by virtue of its vibration. This is the essence of the metaphysics of prosperity: Things that are similar vibrate similarly and therefore they are attracting each other. They add to each other and for a time vibrate identical frequencies until intrinsic conditions change. The metaphysics of Creation is that it is all about 'attraction.' Whatever it is that you're looking at or talking about, whatever it is that has your attention has got you offering a vibrational signal. Consider that sometimes the words you use

71

sound positive but the inner vibration is negative. There is no correspondence between the two but they need to be balanced and congruent.

For example, many people want to be loved from a place of not feeling loved. The feeling of not being loved is a contradictory signal to the desire for love. When your thoughts and feelings vibrationally match your desires, your energy is purely aligned. Then the manifestation takes place because there is little or no opposition to it.

CO-CREATION

Co-creation and 'being alive' is about activating and creating a vibration within you, and then the Law of Attraction takes care of the rest. This is the bridge between psychology and spiritual practice that can transform your life.

We all possess a natural and precise measuring tool - our 'emotional body,' which is always accurate and never failing, to assist you in knowing how you are activating and directing your vibrational signal, how you feel. Your 'emotions' are the connecting link between your inner and outer world.

The reason this broader aspect of yourself communicates to you in terms of 'emotion' is because it's virtually impossible to transmit a thought and receive a thought simultaneously. However, you can offer a thought and receive a feeling response relative to that thought concurrently.

This system was divinely designed so that the impulses you feel in terms of negative or positive emotion will assist you in knowing which thoughts contradict your true desires.

POSITIVE EMOTION

Positive emotion always means you are a vibrational match to your desire and the attraction is in the process of being implemented. Conversely, negative emotion means you are in the process of attracting something you don't want. There is no 'Law of Exclusion' – there is only Law of Attraction.

Your inner self knows this and gives you a negative emotion to alert you that you are including something in your vibration that is contradictory to your desire, and that's what keeps you from giving the pure signal (with aligned positive thought and emotion) that would bring you rapidly to a full manifestation of your desires.

If you have a negative emotion and you are not heeding the guidance from within, your problem, by Law of Attraction will only get bigger. If you still ignore it, the condition will continue to get worse until it gets so big you are forced to make a different choice.

By understanding the metaphysics of the Law of Attraction you can realize your former limitations; to catch negative emotion as it is happening in the earlier stages, and thereby redirect your attention toward what you really want, which serves to maintain your vibrational alignment toward its manifestation. Authenticity, being true to yourself, centered in who you really are and expressing your true self more completely are of utmost importance in manifesting abundance and wealth in your life.

To change the structure of your reality, rediscover your inner wisdom and power. Live authentically. Be yourself. By doing so, you can break through your fears, blockages, and limitations. The result will be that you will grow more often through love and joy, rather than pain and struggle. As growth is through relationships, compassion for one another is vital.

Therefore, it is important to clarify your personal and global visions, listen to the 'whispers' from within, the Inner Voice, and make your dreams come true, as you awaken to the magic and wonder of this incredible journey we call life.

Pie Chart Quadrants

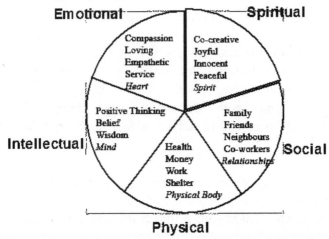

METAPHYSICS OF MONEY

Money is only one small aspect of the vast totality of physical, intellectual, emotional, social and spiritual components that create true prosperity. But let's take a closer look at 'money,' that which seems to captivate so much attention and concern.

The etymology of the word 'metaphysics' reveals that it was first used in English around 1387, meaning 'a branch or speculation which deals with the first causes of things.' It is derived from middle Latin 'metaphysica' and from Medieval Greek 'metaphysika' and originally meant 'the works after physics.'

The word 'money' c. 1290 means 'coinage, currency' and is derived from Old French 'moneie' from Latin 'moneta' meaning 'mint, coinage' and from 'moneta' a title for the Roman goddess Juno, in or near whose temple money was coined. Juno was the Roman goddess who protected the special counsellor of the state. To make money 'earn pay' is first attested in 1457.

Therefore 'the metaphysics of money' in essence would mean 'the first causes of earning or making money' and 'the works after these first causes.'

Gia Combs-Ramirez explains in her article 'Metaphysics of Money' that most people consider, either consciously or subconsciously, money as a measure of life force. A common misperception is the belief that by expending life force, by means of working, a person receives a certain amount of materialized money in return. To view it only in this way is to lock into a very limiting belief system of haves and have-nots, according to how much money you possess. In reality, there is so much more to true prosperity than just the amount of money you possess. However, above and beyond the associations between life force, work, and amount of money materialized, a deeper psychological perspective about the metaphysics of money is available showing why it may flow or not flow in abundance in your life.

For instance, many people may in fact project their unresolved psychological issues onto money. These psychological issues may include religion, sex, power, family, unresolved karma, self-worth and a host of many other issues. As an example, if you feel unworthy of love then you may hinder yourself to 'receive.' If you have low self-esteem you may get your primary sense of self worth from a dollar value amount. Another example of unresolved psychological issues affecting the flow of money in your life would be if you energetically give off the signal that you are unworthy, thus ensuring you aren't paid your worth.

When you energetically work with money, you tend to mistakenly perceive at a material level, the source of money as outside yourself. This may result in your life force energy flowing out horizontally in front of you, around your navel chakra, toward a vibrational form that you consider to be the source of the money you desire, such as governments, bosses, corporations, parents or to whomever you give away your power. Energetically this creates a reversed flow to your growth. To correct this reversed flow, and create a positive flow, you must remember that the 'power' comes from within yourself.

Activation of your inner energy centres would be helpful in creating an increased flow toward enhanced prosperity.

A more correct perception to facilitate a full manifestation of abundance is as follows: Gia Combs-Ramirez explains that metaphysically money represents a form of energy from the Creator Source. This energy flow, at its purest essence is that which activates/nourishes life or vital force energy within us. The misperception is that there is not enough for everyone.

Alternatively, an enlightened view reveals that we live in an infinitely abundant universe with plenty of energy for all of us. When this concept is truly known throughout every fibre of your being then money is perceived more clearly. Money transforms from a materialistic level to a spiritualized one. It becomes an expression of life force instead of a measure of it.

Metaphysically, in order to have greater amounts of money in your life, simply activate and thereby increase the flow of vital life force energy throughout your energy centres and thereby your entire body.

Your intentions will decide the form of expression that the life force energy takes. Also helpful in creating increased life force energy is joy and reverence for life. Interestingly, when you express joy, reverence and gratitude, increased abundance, including money will naturally follow.

INCREASING THE FLOW OF MONEY, ABUNDANCE AND WELL BEING IN YOUR LIFE

Based on research by Gia Combs-Ramirez, you can easily integrate a practice into your daily life that will assist in increasing your flow of money, abundance and well being. life.

First, maintain an attitude of gratitude; be grateful for everything already in your life. The good that you have already manifested in your life you have co-created from life force energy. Where attention goes, energy flows. So if you are only noticing a lack of money in your life then you are affirming a sense of lack in your reality. By doing so, you reduce the flow of energy through you, thereby blocking abundance in your life. Alternatively, express sincere appreciation from your heart to the Creator Source for all that you have.

Secondly, develop conscious awareness of what nourishes you spiritually. From what sources do you receive spiritual sustenance? This might be a foundation, spiritual organization, non-profit foundation, institution or person. Forms of thankful acknowledgement of spiritual nourishment are to donate of your time, talents, or treasures (money) to assist in affirming reverence for life.

Thirdly, practice generosity. An example of creating an increased energetic life force flow is to 'pay if forward' or to be sincerely generous by donating of your time, talents, or treasures (money) at the beginning of each month to a worthy cause. By doing so you are making a powerful statement that you are thriving and not just surviving. The practice of generosity opens your channels for increased abundance for yourself and others. You then attract money and also other forms of abundance while easing the suffering of others and assisting them onward in their journey into greater abundance.

Finally, practice conscious intentionality, by adding 'intentions' to your money. So simply link your cheques or money to your spiritual values with an *intention* and then send it on its way.

Interestingly, some further insights into prosperity and increasing the flow of abundance in your life are highlighted in an article called 'The Great Lie of Scarcity and the Three Toxic Myths' by Judith Morgan. She reminds you of the importance of letting go of three critical misconceptions in order to increase the flow of abundance and prosperity, and make the Law of Attraction work for you. The first myth to let go of is the belief that *there is not enough* or *I am not enough.* The second myth to let go of is that *more is better*, which is not necessarily true. The third myth to release is the mistaken belief *that's just the way it is*, since it doesn't necessarily have to be; that's just your present choice.

CONCLUSION

In conclusion, to understand the great potential of true prosperity it is important to clearly know that there is truly enough of everything, for everyone to have enough. Also, perceive yourself in terms of: *I am enough, I have always had enough and I will always have enough, and that's so true.*

Finally, true prosperity involves clearly knowing that sufficiency is *making a difference with what you already have* and therefore you can be *grateful* and *satisfied* with your life today, what is presently manifest now and each moment as it manifests, just the way it is, and therefore to work with what is.

Further insights into the nature of true prosperity reveal that abundance includes the manifestation of money as only one small aspect of wealth. *Wealth* in essence means well-being. To experience true, total well-being in your life is to manifest holistic wealth that includes well-being in terms of physical, intellectual, emotional, social and spiritual wealth.

Furthermore, *true prosperity* is the strength, faith, and character qualities to face any life situation that you may find yourself in, as you continue on in your joyful co-creative life journey: Together with the love and care that you receive from your Higher Power each step along the way. True prosperity is the life journey of wellness and the creative action taken toward manifesting increased abundance for the benefit of you, your family, relatives, friends, humanity and the environment, so that together you may co-create a world that works for everyone.

KEY POINTS

- True prosperity is composed of many elements of physical, intellectual, emotional, social and spiritual well-being. Some examples of true prosperity are good health based on healthy eating and living. Fulfilling relationships with family, spouse, friends, neighbours, co-workers, associates and a sense of community. Rewarding career, sustained mental, emotional and spiritual growth, as well as worthy material possessions, along with financial wealth.

- Positive moods and feeling happy can assist in creating more positive life experiences.

- Thought and emotion are two primary aspects of holistic prosperity/abundance that influence the process of the Law of Attraction.

- The metaphysics of the Law of Attraction is that everything that vibrates in harmony with everything else comes together.

- Co-creation is all about activating and creating a vibration within us and then allowing the Law of Attraction to take care of the rest.

- To create a positive flow and manifest abundance you must remember that the *power* comes from within yourself.

- Metaphysically, money represents a flow of energy from the Creator Source. This energy flow activates the vital force within you.

- We live in an infinitely abundant universe.

- Affirm abundance, be generous, and be grateful; add intentions to your money.

- True prosperity is the inherent strength, faith and character qualities to face any life situation that you may find yourself in, together with love and care received from your Higher Power.

- To feel loved, along with positive self-esteem, will assist in activating your inner power centres and increasing the flow of life force resulting in enhanced manifestation of abundance and true prosperity in your life.

EXERCISE

Create an increased energetic life force flow as a practice integrated into your daily life, by means of 'paying it forward' and practicing generosity.

Some examples of practical exercises to increase your energetic life force flow are:

- Generously donate some of your time, talent or treasure (one possibility being money) at the beginning of each month to a worthy cause (for example: to ease world hunger or poverty or to assist the homeless).
- Decide to seek out and consciously become aware of assistance that a family member, relative, friend, co-worker, or acquaintance may need and offer help without waiting for them to ask for it.
- Do a small good deed daily.
- Promote a spirit of teamwork, community, and co-operation rather than competition and struggle against one another. We're all in this together!
- Find ways within your means to ease suffering.
- Have an attitude of gratitude and work with what is presently manifested in your life. Understand great accomplishments begin with small steps.
- Know that as compassionate energy flows then abundance grows helping to create a world that works for everyone.

PROSPERITY QUOTES

Light tomorrow with today
– **Elizabeth Barrett Browning**.

The secret of health for both mind and body is not to mourn for the past, worry about the future, or anticipate troubles, but to live in the present moment wisely and earnestly
– **Buddha**.

Failure is in a sense the highway to success, as each discovery of what is false leads us to seek earnestly after what is true
– **John Keats**

A wise man turns chance into good fortune
– **Thomas Fuller**

There is no way to prosperity, prosperity is the way
– **Wayne Dyer**

With realization of one's potential and self-confidence in one's ability, one can build a better world
– **Dalai Lama**.

We are always prosperous to the degree that we are expressing love, joy, health and abundance in our lives
– **Catherine Ponder**.

TOP 'TRUE PROSPERITY' QUESTIONS

The following questions are designed to enhance and clarify your understanding of true prosperity. You have to be able to ask the right questions in order to get to more complete and holistic perspectives about prosperity. How can you develop true prosperity in your life if you only assumed that you understand what true prosperity means, when in fact you may only be focusing on one small aspect of prosperity?

By reflecting on the following questions and answering them for yourself you may see which important aspects of prosperity that you truly understand and conversely which areas need further development, consideration, research, thought or deepened understanding. We suggest that every so often you answer this list of true prosperity questions and compare your answers over time. By doing so you will be able to become aware of and ascertain how your understanding of true prosperity has deepened or become more holistic and clear.

TOP 'TRUE PROSPERITY' QUESTIONS

PERSONAL EXERCISE

Write down the following questions on a paper and with some reflection and careful consideration answer the questions to the best of your present ability. Repeat this exercise a few months or a year later to become increasingly aware of your own personal growth in understanding of true prosperity, which directly affects your ability to make the Law of Attraction work for you. Also, consider some of the following answers from professionals in the field, which brings further light on the process of transformation and abundance in your life.

QUESTIONS

1. What does well-being mean to you?
2. How do you create well-being in your life?
3. How do you define wealth?
4. What is one most important key for wealth creation?
5. What is the role of a higher purpose or mission in your life?
6. How does living with purpose connect with the law of attraction?
7. Does the law of attraction involve giving and receiving?
8. How would you define a co-creative universe?
9. How does co-creation with the universe and others influence the law of attraction?
10. Can we experience blocks in manifestation? If so how can we remove them?
11. Do you have a key message about manifesting prosperity that others need to remember?

SOME FURTHER INSIGHTS INTO TRUE PROSPERITY

True prosperity is the accumulation of material wealth yet is also so very much more. Five key elements that true prosperity is composed of involve manifestation of physical, intellectual, emotional, social and spiritual abundance.

When considering all of the key elements that are each equally important to the creation of true prosperity, you quickly come to realize that money, material wealth, and abundance directed toward yourself only are a small aspect of *true* prosperity.

PHYSICAL

Physical prosperity and abundance includes good health, financial abundance, having a skill/career that is fulfilling and rewarding, comfortable, quiet and bright shelter along with a healthy lifestyle inclusive of proper exercise, proper breathing, rest & relaxation, proper diet, positive thinking and meditation.

INTELLECTUAL

Intellectual prosperity includes meta-cognition, the process of self-reflection, positive thinking and clarity of mind, also peace of mind, along with personal growth through intellectual learning.

EMOTIONAL

Emotional prosperity is inclusive of strongly developed character qualities such as peacefulness, joy, being responsible, along with compassion and fearlessness.

SOCIAL

Social prosperity and abundance is the creation and maintenance of ongoing well-balanced relationships that are enjoyable and mutually beneficial with family, friends, co-workers, community and internationally.

SPIRITUAL

Reflective of spiritual abundance and prosperity is an ongoing co-creative relationship with your Higher Self that results in the development of your inner virtues that strengthens your good character qualities and enables you to overcome fear with a strong and steady faith.

Spiritual abundance also enables you to focus on and live into the highest good for all concerned with a spirit of gratitude. Also, you are able to remain true to yourself; to be the unique individual that you are and to express your inner gifts enabling you to take action that assists in creating a better world.

TRUE PROSPERITY SELF TEST

Answer the following questions as accurately as possible to determine the percentage of prosperity that you already manifest in your life. Also verify the areas that may need additional focus in order to manifest more of your abundance and true prosperity.

Simply answer yes or no for the following questions:

PHYSICAL

1. Do you have good physical health?
2. Have you manifest abundance financially?
3. Do you have a rewarding and fulfilling skill or career?
4. Do you have a quiet, bright comfortable shelter to live in?
5. Do you live a healthy lifestyle?

INTELLECTUAL

1. Do you self-reflect on your experiences
   to gain deeper understanding?
2. Do you think positively?
3. Do you maintain clarity of mind?
4. Do you have peace of mind?
5. Do you experience ongoing intellectual learning?

EMOTIONAL

Have you developed the following character qualities?
1. Are you peaceful?
2. Are you joyful?
3. Are you responsible toward yourself and others?
4. Are you actively compassionate toward yourself and others?
5. Do you live your life without fear?

SOCIAL

Have you developed and manifested the following mutually beneficial relationships?
1. With your spouse, children, relatives?
2. With your friends?
3. With your co-workers?
4. In your community?
5. International relations?

SPIRITUAL

Have you developed a co-creative relationship with your Higher Self (Universe, Energy Centres, the Divine, God)?
1. Have you developed inner virtues and strong positive character qualities, such as compassion, generosity, persistence, focus etc.?
2. Have you overcome fears and thereby established a steady faith?
3. Do you express an attitude of gratitude?
4. Are you true to yourself and your unique individuality?
5. Are you expressing your inner gifts in daily life?

Give yourself one point for each question that you gave an answer of 'yes.' Then multiply your score by 4 to determine the percentage of prosperity that you presently manifest in your life.

Also, it will become clear as to your areas of strengths and weakness in relation to the true prosperity manifest in your life. For each section of the pie you can multiply your score by 20 to determine the percentage of prosperity presently manifest in that particular section.

The True Prosperity Self Test can be repeated a few months later to determine the amount of progress you have made and to be clearly grateful, since everything can serve as a learning experience, and to determine what areas of your True Prosperity Pie that require further attention and work.

Congratulations on the true prosperity that you've already manifested in your life thus far. Sincere best wishes for the true prosperity that you may manifest in the future as you continue on your journey with the Law of Attraction and learn more of how to make it work for you.

Bibliography for Chapter 3

Baldwin Howe, John: *The Common Sense*

Berg, Yehuda: *True Prosperity: How to Have Everything*

Combs-Ramirez, Gia: *Metaphysics of Money*

Ellison, Michael R: *10 Keys to Create Wellness*

Morgan, Judith: *The Great Lie of Scarcity and the Three Toxic Myths*

Smith, Gerry, D: *What is True Prosperity?*

Valdman, Edourd: *Jews and Money*

Words of Wisdom...

After reaching new levels of awareness we are continually drawn into circumstances within the physical world to apply our remembrances, integrate them and offer this new awareness to others, thus manifesting Heaven on Earth
The Seven Initiations of the Spiritual Path
- Michael Mirdad

Take the first step in faith
You don't have to see the whole staircase
Just take the first step
- Dr. Martin Luther King Jr.

As you begin to take action toward the fulfillment of your goals and dreams, you must realize that not every action will be perfect. Not every action will produce the desired result. Not every action will work. Making mistakes, getting it almost right, and experimenting to see what happens are all part of the process of eventually getting it right
– Jack Canfield

Chapter **4**

The Energy of Symbols

Thinking in Images

Ananda K. Coomaraswamy describes symbolism as 'the art of thinking in images.' Our thinking is moved by images and some images are more powerful than others. The most compelling are those that have a deep personal significance or meaning. You are drawn to certain objects at particular times in your life, especially during periods of change or transition.

Symbols are a wonderful tool for making the Law of Attraction work in your life because they allow you to activate different areas of your life through intention. You can also use symbols to express your deepest desires in concrete terms, so that your intention is brought into concrete form. An essential metaphor for human faculties is found in the Five Elements, depicted traditionally as a star or pentacle where Spirit is the head of a person, Air and Water as the outstretched arms, and Earth and

Fire as the legs. The five elements are an ancient symbol central to making the Law of Attraction work for you.

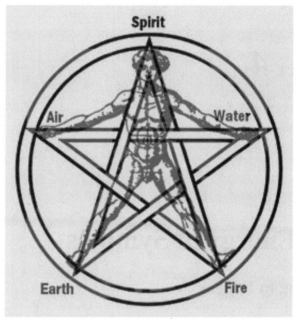

The Five Elements

Each element is related to energy within you, a particular manifestation in your life as the following chart shows:

Element	*Manifestation*
Spirit	Spiritual
Air	Psychological
Fire	Relational
Water	Intuitional
Earth	Physical

These elements in varied combinations are found universally in different cultures and times. The ancient Greeks believed in these elements and the same essential Five Elements are also found in India, China, Japan, and modern-day Wicca and Paganism.

Each element is connected with certain traits and invested with symbolic meaning. Symbols are used to express intention through an object of where you want to grow. You can use symbols for greater abundance in any part of your life.

If you want to increase spiritual growth, symbolized by Spirit element, you can activate it through understanding and using symbols in your daily life. You can create spiritual space in your home through a place of meditation, reflection and calmness. Many people have a room, part of a room or shrine dedicated to this purpose. By invoking symbols in that space, you can make your desire for peace, centeredness, harmony and spiritual growth clear to yourself and to the Universe.

For some people, the preferred area of growth is mental clarity, clear purpose, and greater knowledge and wisdom found in the element of Air. Air is symbolically connected to thought as both are fast-moving and changeable. A study, a library or a space dedicated to learning in the home allows for this desire to manifest into concrete physical reality. Symbols attached to learning can amplify the desire for growth in knowledge.

Yet, even with learning you always feel the need for close relationships, which leads to the relational Fire element. Fire since ancient times has been associated with emotions, since both represent heat and warmth. Emotions that bring you into closer relationship with others through love, empathy and compassion are developed within your heart. Your closeness with relationships is expressed in the shared spaces in your home: The Family Room, Living Room and Dining Rooms, where we interact, play together, watch TV or movies, welcome guests and where we share food. This is where your desire for companionship and belonging finds concrete expression. In this communal atmosphere, through symbols you can communicate your desire for friendship, strong family bonds, and welcome others into your home.

Besides closeness with family and friends, you also want to share your life with a significant other. If you are already in a satisfying relationship, then you may want to grow closer with your partner. The intention for passion, sensuality and desire is represented by the water element. Yet as with water your raw passions and drives need to be directed in productive directions through cleansing and willpower just as water purifies and through steady force makes progress.

The final part of the Law of Attraction is expressed in your manifestation on the physical plane. This will depend on your foundations, actions and attitudes. Manifestation is a lot like a pine tree, whose seed contains the full expression of the tree. The development of an individual pine tree and the final form it takes depends on a number of factors. The quality of the soil is like the family in which you were born and how you were raised. For some the soil is poor for others it is rich. The terrain is like the geographical area in which you are born, which shapes your opportunities and challenges in life. The sun and wind are like endowed gifts, talents and Divine Grace, which give sustenance and growth. The pine like you reacts to its surroundings and circumstances. It bends and twists to grow towards the sun just as you want to express your highest intentions. Unlike the pine, you are able to consciously participate in your growth through awareness and become co-creators — the Universe working through you and you vibrating your awareness to the Universe.

We have talked a lot about symbols. But what exactly is a symbol?

Definition of a Symbol

When Homer and Alexander, two close friends who lived in Ancient Greece, parted they broke a coin between them. They agreed that anyone who had the other half of the coin was entitled to hospitality between their houses. So whenever they, one of their friends or a family member returned, they would present the other half. If the halves fit together then that person was entitled to hospitality in their houses.

From this fitting together of two halves the word symbol, *symbolon* in Greek or 'to throw together,' is derived. So a symbol is an object or image that brings or throws together two halves. Symbols often come up at points where consciousness is unable to navigate the tension and mystery contained in opposites. When you cannot describe something, then you connect it to something else.

A symbol connects an abstract idea to a tangible image, so that the unknown and mysterious can be understood by a known tangible image. Symbols can bridge the gap between surface understanding to deep wisdom.

A metaphor compares things on the basis of an underlying similarity between them. All symbols at their root are a metaphor. Through correspondence between two entities, symbols express the underlying unity between heaven and earth, male and female and spirit and matter.

A common metaphor is life as a journey and this is vividly expressed in symbolic images in art, literature and cinema where along the journey of life we are faced with challenges that we need to go through in order to grow.

The pop song *He Ain't Heavy, He's My Brother* by The Hollies, illustrates the journey metaphor:

It's a long, long road
From which there is no return.
While we're on the way to there
Why not share?

A symbol is rooted in strong emotions imbuing an object with new textures, colours and meanings. Symbols as a basis for shared experience, have a powerful affect on our awareness. In the words of Carl Jung, the Swiss psychiatrist who explored the depth of the human psyche: 'The psychological mechanism that transforms energy is the symbol.' A symbol unlocks energies throughout your energetic body along circular discs called chakras in India and sefiroth in Jewish Kabbalah. Human beings are predisposed to make symbols as shown in prehistoric cave paintings found in Europe, Africa, Asia and Australia. Symbols are commonly used in art, literature and religion.

Symbols are transformers of energy, taking the merely conceptual and giving it a container, a focal point. They are hard-wired because the structure of the brain is designed to produce images and emotions — the very ingredients needed to create symbols.

St Paul in Romans 1:20 expresses the way symbols bridge the gap between visible and invisible reality: 'For since the creation of the world God's invisible qualities—God's eternal power and divine nature—have been clearly seen, being understood from what has been made.'

Symbols arise from contacting with outer reality and our capacity to find meaning in the process. In working with them we need a child-like curiosity and openness. Still not all objects are symbols, some are only signs.

Signs and Symbols

A sign is clearly defined by consensus but a symbol expresses something beyond its literal meaning. So the meaning of a stop sign is agreed upon by consensus but the symbol of a cross represents something beyond itself.

In Christianity, the cross represents the sacrifice of Christ with great emotional intensity for a believer. So a symbol is a word or image that implies something beyond its concrete meaning and something connected to and eliciting deep human emotions.

Signs abound in math, science and information processing where replication of results is important. Symbols are common in humanities, religion and art where connections between ideas are highly valued.

The use of symbols allows us to expand our understanding through a dynamic tool and by it we can make the Law of Attraction work for us. We need to play with symbols in a carefree manner just like children.

Childhood Curiosity

When you are with young kids, you realize how their awareness of symbols and signs is like a great insight. Deborah's three-year old grandson, Logan, who loves going for a car ride, always reminds you that red means 'stop' and green means 'go.' For him signs are a new discovery, so he is fascinated by them.

When you work with symbols in this book, we want you to have the same curiosity and sense of discovery. Learn to play with symbols and become fascinated by how you can use them in your own life whether at work or at home. The following discussion on shapes can help in arousing your creative play with symbols.

What Do The Shapes Say?

Shapes can often symbolize the flow of energy around you. So when you place an object of a particular shape in your living room, bedroom, or office, it communicates something. Different shapes say different things, so selecting the right one to place in your space is conducive to manifest abundance in the area associated with that space.

The list of possible shapes and their symbolic associations is endless, yet the basic purpose of symbols remains the same: To attract growth and abundance in your life. The Law of Attraction as presented in other books is limited in terms of human faculties and growth. To make the Law of Attraction work for you, you need to expand it.

○	### The Circle The circle represents Spirit as infinite, universal and sacred. It is the most widely used shape, without a beginning or end. The sun is round, natural cycles are circular and a ring symbolizes everlasting love is also round. Found in vases, bowls and open vessels
●	### The Dot The dot is the centre-point, the point of creation, from which everything started. It depicts the origin of life and the universe. It shows a return to the original unity before creation. Found in mandalas, diagrams and the metaphor of the seed.
⊙	### Circle with Dot This represents becoming inwardly centered. The dot is like the axle of a wheel while the circle is like the rim. At the outer circle is movement, while at the central dot we find stillness or peace. This image represents connecting to the core of your being. Found in mandalas and diagrams.
▬	### Horizontal Line Horizontal line; passive, static state. Flat objects encourage retaining energy instead of free movement. Found in long tables, shelves
▌	### Vertical Line A vertical line represents active, dynamic state. This is one of the reasons that Gothic cathedrals and skyscrapers inspire awe. Found also in tall trees, poles and chimneys.

☐	**Square or Rectangle** Square or rectangle: containment of energy, since they allow people to orient themselves in a space, which is why most homes and rooms are designed this way. Squares and rectangles offer safety and stability.
△	**Upward Triangle** This shows evolution of spiritual qualities where energies are directed upward. Yoga and Indian spiritual traditions tend to emphasize lower to higher evolution along chakras or energy centres symbolically located along the spine. Found in pyramid shapes and on the reverse of US one-dollar bill.
▽	**Downward Triangle** This shows downward movement of energies into the creation. It is involved with manifestation of possibilities and desires on earth. The movement in Kabbalah in this direction. Found in diagram of Tree of Life, Chakras and Mandalas.
✡	**Two Intermingling Triangles** This is of course the Jewish Star of David but it is also a symbol of two dynamic forces working together of heaven and earth, male and female and light and dark.
✝	**The Cross** Best-known symbol of Christianity, representing crucifixion of Jesus Christ. It is also an ancient symbol of life, immortality and union of heaven and earth.

Expansion of Understanding

Previous works on the Law of Attraction have focused on the importance of developing positive thoughts and feeling good. These resources have offered valuable insights on the Law of

Attraction, integrated into this book. We are also expanding on the Law by offering new tools to manifest your desires.

One of the tools is the Kabbalistic Tree of Life, which maps energy centres throughout the human body. *Kabbalah* or Jewish Mysticism offers a system of profound wisdom as shown by the *Tree of Life*.

The Energy Centres or Spheres

The Tree of Life symbol shows three pillars. On the left side is the pillar connected with the feminine principle and the one on the right is masculine. These two columns represent the idea of *polarities*, commonly found throughout the world of religion, art and literature. We will explore the tension between polarities elsewhere, since their *integration* leads to harmony and balance.

However, the primary focus of this book is *The Middle Pillar*, which integrates the energies of the other two pillars. This Pillar is most relevant to manifestation and its five key circles are the basis for manifestation in this book. These circles are centres of energy, which when blocked impede the flow of universal energy called *chi* in China and *prana* in India. When these centres are activated through conscious intention, then energy is released for well-being in all areas of life. The activation of that energy at each centre is essential to manifest the Law of Attraction.

The process of activation occurs at each energy centre or sphere starting from the top centre of Spirit, then moving down to Air, Fire, Water and Earth spheres. These centres are called *sefiroth* in Kabbalah, similar to Indian *chakras* found in yoga.

One of the main differences between the Kabbalistic system and yoga is the direction of energetic flow. In yoga with a traditional emphasis on spiritual development, the movement is from lower to upper centres. In Kabbalah the energy goes down, since Jewish mysticism attempts to understand the process of *manifestation* of Spirit into creation. For our purpose, this downward flow is most important to make the Law of Attraction work in your life.

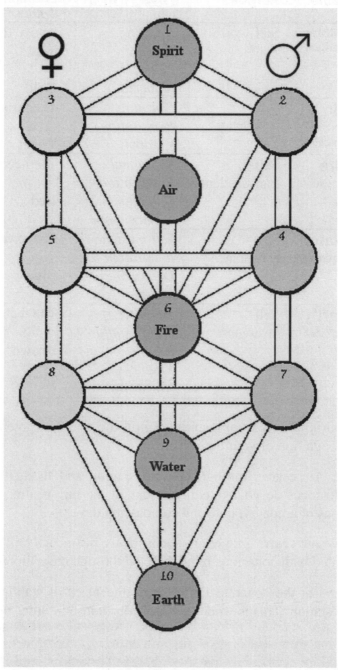

The Tree of Life

Name	Purpose	Description	Location Colour
Spirit Spiritual	Self-worth	*Uplifting, Joyous, Peaceful, Innocent*	Above the head **Gold**
Air Psycho- logical	Self- confidence	*Learning, Exploration, Wisdom*	The throat **Violet**
Fire Relational	Self- transcendence	*Relational, Purification, Compassion, Service, Love*	The heart **Red**
Water Intuitional	Self- acceptance	*Self-mastery, Integration, Determination, Desire*	The navel **Blue**
Earth Physical	Self- awareness	*Stability, Manifestation, Health, Finances, Nurturing*	The feet **Brown**

The journey starts from inspiring Spirit, the centre of potentiality and recognition of your inner worth.

At the Air centre, through conscious mind and thoughts, you learn to focus on your intention. Next, at the Fire centre, higher emotions of empathy, love and compassion develop.

The Water centre is where subconscious instinctual drives are integrated with conscious mind directed through the willpower.

You end at the concrete Earth centre the place of stability and manifestation. This is where you get your house in order through awareness.

Activation

As you move into a centre and element associated with it, you are looking to activate the energy there through using tools and techniques suitable for that area. This will often require looking at potential blocks to the flow of energy in a given sphere.

At the Spirit centre a primary block is associated with feelings of being directionless, life lacking meaning, or general confusion and disorientation. The root of these feelings is a lack of connection to your centre where peace and inspiration reside. One of the means to connect to your centre involves visualization exercises that use symbols that represent the inner centre-point such as Mandalas, Yantras and various other circular designs.

When we start from our peaceful centre then our energies are open, yielding and relaxed. The tense, agitated energy that often characterizes our daily activity is let go. The Law of Attraction begins with peace, so that the path you follow will lead to peace.

A block may arise from psychological conditioning at the Air centre where your ingrained thought patterns block you from growth. Negative thought patterns can reinforce cynicism, disbelief and inaction. So through meditation and awareness, you can examine these thoughts and release them, allowing for self-confidence and belief to replace them. When you believe in yourself and the Universe, your psychological resistance to transformation through the Law of Attraction is reduced and in time with practice eliminated.

While the development of conscious intention is important, subconscious motivations at the Fire centre also need to be explored. Otherwise the disharmony between the conscious and subconscious mind will sabotage our efforts. Many positive individuals who have worked with the Law have often been frustrated because of this unexamined conflict. Even with the best intentions, your deep-seated emotions have great power and merely trying to put a lid on them or forcefully applying surface-level intentions will not work, since the emotions always win out.

We need to instead examine the emotions, fully engage with them, acknowledge them and bring them to conscious awareness.

Some of these powerful emotions are aspects of you that are hidden from conscious awareness. They are aspects that you find uncomfortable, shadowy and confusing. So the conscious wants to deny them but by accepting them, we can release a lot of the pent up energy taken up by them. We need to be aware that some of these charged emotions are locked away because the hurt and pain associated with them is too difficult to bring to the surface.

In cases of extreme repression associated with past abuse, the help of a counsellor or therapist is essential to work through the emotions and to create healing. Your emotions can undergo a transformation as you move from anger, blame and coldness to forgiveness, responsiveness and compassion at the Fire centre.

The Water centre is where our strongest urges, passions and drives reside. These drives can range from achievement, sexual or competitive urges. When this sphere is powerful in a person, you will find charisma or a charged energy in them. While this is a powerful centre, you need to channel the energies into a productive direction.

The powerful images and symbols associated with this area are those of transformation, conversion from purely animal instincts to a willpower that can direct energies for growth. For those who experience inaction or indecision in their life, recharging this sphere is an important step toward manifestation.

The final sphere, Earth, is where you take action and where all your work comes to fruition. This is where infinity touches physical reality, where your desires are balanced with natural ecosystems, and where you look to concretely manifest your plans. Management of money and helping it to grow are essential to create your foundation here. You also check your progress and make changes to enhance growth. On Earth, you at times need to accept what you cannot change; those things that are outside of your control.

Through activation spheres along the Middle Pillar are energized and integrated in order to progress toward integrity, wholeness and ultimately manifesting more completely in your life.

Each sphere is activated through intentionality expressed through specific tools including holistic understanding of wealth, symbols and useful exercises. Your understanding of the centre in terms of its energy and purpose is important. Then you release any blocked energy and integrate the centre through your journey at each one and the element associated with it. You activate and energize each centre with specific exercises and techniques.

The spheres are activated regardless of whether you experience them and their attributes, such as, elemental associations, colours or location in the human body as real or symbolic.

An Integrative Approach

Previous material on the Law of Attraction has primarily focused on positive thinking related to the Fire and Air centres as is evident with a number of prosperity teachers. This approach may be exactly what you need to make the Law of Attraction work for you. However, some of you may require another approach in order to manifest abundance in your life. Some prosperity teachers do in fact integrate aspects of other Energy centres beyond Fire and Air into their teachings, as is evident with Dr. Joe Vitale, Dr. Michael Mirdad and other writers. We suggest that you focus on what works for you and integrate it into your life.

We provide a simple formula for prosperity:

Spirit
Believe
Activate
Receive

The above formula is based on a process of activating each of your five Energy centres. This activation process creates a balanced and synchronistic flow of energy throughout your inner being that flows into your life experience. Everyday use of symbols to empower your intentions, activation of all five Vital Energy Centres, and mindfulness of the corresponding Five Elements of the Universe are all incorporated in order to attract more of what you want into your life.

You are expanding the Law to include steps that were previously missing from attraction. This book overcomes the gap inherent in some previous approaches by developing an integrated approach that encompasses all five Vital Spheres.

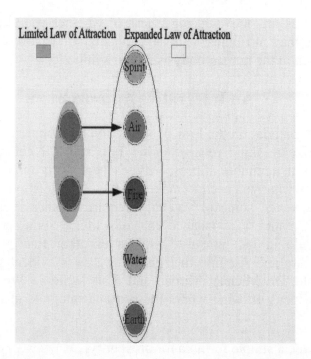

The illustration shows the Law of Attraction has previously largely focused on Air and Fire centres related to thoughts and emotions. This limited focus explains why the Law has not always worked in the past. An expanded approach encompasses the Five Elements, offering greater potential for manifesting success from an expanded perspective.

What Matters is You

Symbols are powerful because through their use the individual is transformed, yet symbols are truly powerful when they have personal meaning. You have different social, political, religious and psychological experiences. So your use of symbols will vary and we have to trust those symbols that elicit strong emotional reaction from us – those that resonate within our being.

A symbol takes on personal meaning: A sword is viewed differently by a soldier, a priest, a collector or a poet. The symbolic meaning of an object encountered in a dream or in waking life offers many insights but its real meaning lies within you. Personal reflection and examination are an important part of working with symbols as you integrate subconscious material with conscious intentions. When you pay attention only to conscious expectations, then subconscious intuition is neglected, which often finds release in symbolic imagery of dreams.

You need the guidance of the subconscious in order to know your real motivations. Where do your dreams, wishes and deep-seated desires want you to go and are these subconscious promptings consistent with conscious intention?

Symbols are both universal and personal. Universal in that symbols go back to prehistoric times and personal because you relate them to your own experiences. For example, a wedding ring as a circular object is connected to the circle, a universal symbol of something infinite and enduring. Yet a wedding ring is connected to intense emotional experiences associated with it. Your own emotional experiences with weddings and marriage can be elicited in the ring. So the ring can communicate messages that are both universal and personal.

Symbols allow us to integrate different aspects of our Being into a whole. We need that integrity to make the Law of Attraction work in life with consistent results. As individuals we can also respond to deeply embedded images called Archetypes, which relate to our own development in all areas of life. That development is necessary in order for us to transmit highest and most powerful vibrations to the Universe.

Archetypes: The Most Powerful Symbols

The most powerful symbols are archetypes, which are original images and metaphors embedded deep within our spirit. They are present in the subconscious and resonate at a core level. Since your brain is hard-wired to conceive images, archetypes arise from deep within your subconscious as collective human memories that are found in all cultures.

So for instance *The Mother* is an archetype, since she is present across many cultures and goes back to the beginning of collective human memory as a figure with great meaning. Her universal image imbedded in your own subconscious also relates her to your personal experiences with your own mother; the one who gave birth, raised and nourished you from infancy to adulthood. You feel a deep relationship with this and other archetypes because they go back to the earliest memories of human experience and they are also tied to your present life. Archetypes are found within each sphere and they form a powerful basis for working with their corresponding sphere.

Spirit: The Centre Within

At the level of Spirit, you find two powerful archetypes. First is the *Self* which represents wholeness through reconciliation of opposites and it is the centre-point where everything emanates in your life. We cannot fully describe it because of its totality, yet it is felt as a real presence — a place of stillness within us. This is often vividly depicted in geometric shapes and symbols including mandalas, derived from Sanskrit for circle.

With intricate design and brilliant colours, mandalas symbolize the movement of energy either outward into creation or inward towards the central point where the Self or Spirit resides. The

106

Kalachakra mandala, derived from Sanskrit *Kala Chakra* meaning 'Time Wheel,' is used in Tibetan Buddhism. Often it is made from coloured sand because after ritual use it is destroyed. Many mandalas are easy to understand but some like the Kalachakra require intricate and esoteric knowledge in order to interpret and use them for self-development. Through a mandala, we can locate ourselves in it in terms of where we are and where we want to go. In the process, we can go from mental distraction to spiritual alertness.

The Kalachakra Sand Mandala

The next archetype connected to Spirit is the ***Child***, which embodies the force of renewal that leads toward wholeness. It is exemplified by figures of Jesus, the young Buddha, Child Nanak and Child Krishna. The image is often of a baby or young child who is vulnerable but still has an inner transformative strength. This archetype is one of hope and a promise of a new start to life where lost purity, innocence and clarity can be regained. When you look at great spiritual teachers from this archetype, you can find great meaning in their life. In turn they can symbolize your own growth, and promise of your own renewal and wholeness. The life of a Divine Child often follows a pattern, where normal dangers are overturned through a greater power.

An example is the Child Nanak who was sleeping while his cattle herd grazed around him. A cobra, normally aggressive in nature, fanned its hood to shade Nanak from the scorching midday sun. We will further explore this Divine Child motif in the chapter on the Spirit Sphere.

The Labyrinth is an ancient symbol commonly found in Europe. It is also a symbol of wholeness, which depicts life journey in the joining of a circle to a spiral shape. The path depicted is meandering, yet it has a purpose – of going to the centre and then returning to the world. Most of us confuse a labyrinth with a maze but they are different, since the labyrinth has only one path without dead-ends. A maze is filled with complex choices but a labyrinth is only concerned with the journey, mental riddles are left as the role of a maze. Many churches have a labyrinth design where the cross is at the centre and it becomes a focal point of meditation as you walk towards the cross you connect to the centre and when you walk out you remember it in your daily life.

Air: The Explorer

The sphere of Air is connected to thought, which can lead to personal growth so long as the thoughts are predominantly positive. An important archetype here is that of an Explorer, since acquisition of knowledge and wisdom are primary motivations of Air. You leave the known and often comfortable boundaries to explore unknown areas. Along your path, you often face your own doubts, anxiety and skepticism.

Most of the images associated with this sphere are male figures, such as the Father, the Messiah, the Sage, the Wizard or the all-encompassing Wise Old Man. However, the figure of the Wise Old Woman can also be present here. Both the Wise Old Man and Woman are a symbol for higher wisdom, which can lead to growth.

Relational Shadows

While your emotional and subconscious life can grow through each centre, before you start you need to examine pre-existing images, otherwise your genuine desires for a soul mate or kindred spirit can be marred by fiery emotions of anger and blame. So you need to recognize and integrate subconscious aspects of your personality into conscious awareness. Through this integration, you will know your desires and you can be consistent in your attraction such as in finding a mate. Part of integration involves encountering shadowy aspects of your subconscious including the anima-animus.

Your image of the opposite gender can take the form of anima for men and animus for women. In Jungian psychology, the anima is the female aspect in a man and the animus is the male aspect in a woman. Both can take dark and light forms in your dreams, attractions and fantasies.

The anima, similar to *femme fatale* in French language, personifies feminine psychological tendencies in a man, including feelings and moods, intuitive hunches, emotional attachment, a connection to nature, and a relationship to the subconscious. The anima is represented through forms of a witch, priestess or any woman who has access to the subconscious or spirit world. The dark side of the anima can create a strong attraction for a particular woman in men usually based on sexual fantasy rather than on an acceptance of her as a real woman.

The animus often takes the form of a sacred conviction in a woman such as with Joan of Arc. It also shows up as cold, obstinate and inaccessible qualities in a woman. In fairy tales and literature, the animus shows up as an animal or monster, including *Beauty and the Beast*. The threatening side of the dark animus shows up as Bluebeard and the Wolf in *Little Red Riding Hood* fairy tale. The attraction to an outlaw, rebel or bad boy is an expression of the animus. Many women as they mature outgrow it but some subconsciously are still attracted to men who exhibit these qualities even without consciously realizing it.

You can honestly recognize how the anima-animus influences your lives in terms of your attractions and whether those attractions are beneficial for your growth. Or are they expressions of undeveloped parts of your own subconscious? If so then you need to work on yourself first. After you become comfortable in your own skin and aware of your own attractions, you can then decide to find your partner in life. Otherwise you will project your own anima or animus impulses onto any potential partner instead of accepting that person for their uniqueness.

One of the best symbols for expressing the integration of masculine and feminine aspects is the Taoist Yin-Yang. It consists of a divided circle with a black and white half but each side contains a small part of the other in a small dot. This indicates that the masculine and feminine energies interact with each other in union.

Yin-Yang or Taijitu

Yin is characterized as dark, soft, feminine and tranquil while yang is described as light, hard, masculine and aggressive. This principle of interdependence of opposing forces lies at the heart of traditional Chinese philosophy, medicine and martial arts.

Yin and Yang are opposite qualities that define each other, together they form a whole. The two halves create transformation as they interact with each other and united they create balance.

The masculine and feminine energies are also represented in the archetype of the Lover. In Hinduism, this is depicted by the union of Shiva-Shakti, Vishnu-Lakshmi and Radha-Krishna. In Christianity, the Church and Christ have a similar relationship, which is why the Church is referred to as the 'bride of Christ.'

The same metaphor also runs through the images of soul-mates, two individuals who at a soul level are one. When people look for a soul-mate, they are either consciously or subconsciously seeking this deeper level of relationship with another person. In order to attract this type of relationship, you want conscious awareness of those qualities that you desire in your mate.

110

The Law of Attraction has focused on intentionality at a conscious level but those surface desires are often cancelled out by subconscious feelings. Since those feelings are powerful, you want to bring them to the surface and recognize how they might influence your conscious intention.

Through this process you will learn to integrate both your heart and your mind. This book will show you how to bring conscious and subconscious motivations into balance, so that you can create true prosperity in all areas of life.

Water: The Animal Within

Some people exude *charisma*. Celebrities, politicians and religious leaders can have this magnetic quality in their appearance or personality along with an ability to inspire people through their communication.

People will watch a particular actor or actress or they will vote for a particular candidate during an election based on the charisma. During the 2008 US Presidential Election, Barack Obama exuded charisma and audiences were captivated by his speeches. He was elected because the majority of American voters were attracted to his charisma and his ideas.

Charisma comes from the Water sphere where powerful impulses are harnessed and developed. The archetype of the animal depicts this transformation from uncontrolled instinctual urges to channelled energies with willpower.

In Chinese and Japanese traditions, the belly is the centre of chi energy. In martial arts, yoga and meditation, breathing is directed to the belly in order to 'pack' the chi there and then to circulate it throughout the body.

When you feel lack of energy, willpower or effort in your life, then you want to work on the Water centre through visualization exercises to stimulate the flow of energy there. By doing so, you are preparing the ground for manifestation at the final centre of Earth.

Earth: Receiving on the Physical Plane

On Earth, you create the foundation for manifestation through the archetype of Mother in her nurturing qualities. You want to nurture all aspects of wealth including money, health and relationships.

As a nurturer, you are moved by compassion, generosity and selflessness to give to others. It also allows you to work for the benefit of your family and those in need in your life through creating a foundation to promote growth, abundance and health.

Sound financial knowledge is also an important part of your growth at this stage. You need to help your money grow and invest it in your future. You also nurture your relationship with Mother Earth, the primary archetype in this sphere, through your desire to leave the planet better for future generations.

Types of Symbols

As long as an image or object ties the literal object with corresponding metaphorical associations, almost anything can be a symbol. The list below shows symbols are found everywhere:

1. Nature – Stones, plants, egg, animals, mountains, valleys, sun, moon, wind, fire, earth, elements, stars
2. Religion – Cross, Star of David, Menorah, Khanda, Lotus, Mandala, Om
3. Myth – Fabled creatures (dragons, phoenix, unicorns), gods, goddesses, national, knights
4. Social – Parents, spouse, men, women
5. Manufactured objects – Homes, rooms, boats, cars, bells, candles, books, wheel
6. National – National animals (bald eagle), flowers, flags, founding fathers/mothers
7. Abstract objects or ideas – Numbers, shapes, colours

Do any of these symbols have particular meaning for you? Are you more inspired by symbols from a particular source listed above — religion, nature, etc? Let us close the chapter with a visualization exercise that incorporates symbols:

Symbol Visualization Exercise

1. Find a quiet place where you can focus your attention
2. Breathe in to the count of 1-2-3-4-5, breathing out 1-2-3-4-5. Make sure your breath goes into your belly. If five is too high for you, you can reduce the count to what is comfortable for you. Take three to five deep breaths until you feel relaxed
3. Now close your eyes and think of a symbol, something that holds personal meaning for you. This can be a religious, natural, archetypal, or any other image
4. Carefully observe how you feel as you visualize the symbol. Do you carry strong emotions connected to what the symbol means to you?

If you're unable to imagine a symbol, that's okay because by the end of this book you will find some that have personal meaning for you and you will learn to use them in your physical space. Those symbols will express your intentions in your surroundings.

Bibliography for Chapter 4

Besserman, Perle	*The Shambhala Guide to Kabbalah and Jewish Mysticism*
Bradler and Scheiner	*Feng Shui Symbols: A User's Handbook*
Cirlot, J.E.	*A Dictionary of Symbols*
De Laszlo, Violet S (editor)	*The Basic Writings of C.G. Jung*
Jung, Carl	*Man and His Symbols*
Kast, Verena	*The Dynamics of Symbols: Fundamentals of Jungian Psychotherapy*
Radaj, DeAnna	*Designing the Life of Your Dreams from the Outside In*

Navigating Through the Energy Centres

The following chapters on five energy centres are abundant with information. We hope they will be a source of inspiration for you.

The chapters are written as a reference guide or resource material. So we suggest that you selectively learn the information and practice those exercises that appeal to you. You don't need to know all the information or practice all the exercises unless your intuition guides you to do so.

Use the material that follows according to your own needs for personal growth, while following it as organized by the various energy centres. This may mean concentrating on some centres where you want more growth and with less emphasis on centres that are already activated. Or you equally work on all of them.

The whole approach is meant to be individualized, so create a personalized practice that is in keeping with your preferences, schedule and focus.

The following chapters offer you the opportunity to select from varied symbols, guided visualizations, exercises, affirmations, energy centre activation techniques and more. So select material that has personal meaning for you.

We wish you joy, wisdom and growth in your personal journey of wealth, success and abundance!

Chapter **5**

The Centre of Spirit: Know Yourself

If you want to accomplish the goals of your life, you have to begin with the spirit
– Oprah Winfrey.

You need to go for inner joy, the inner peace, the inner vision first, and then all the outer things appear
– Marci Shimoff, *The Secret*.

What lies behind us and what lies before us are tiny matters compared to what lies within us
– Ralph Waldo Emerson.

Peace comes from within. Do not seek it without
– Buddha.

Spirit is an invisible force made visible in all life
– Maya Angelou.

What is 'I Am' Awareness?

'I Am' Awareness is being focused on living your life NOW. It is the consciousness by which you feel empowered to transform your life letting go of past regrets or concerns for the future. When you are in 'I Am' state, you know that peace lies within you. It is inexplicable, you cannot say what 'I Am' is, yet you can personally experience that presence.

This may not be as vivid as a burning bush was for Moses, yet in that silence and in an ever-deepening relationship, you can find the presence of 'I Am' touching your life. You were born with this peace and this peace is always accessible to you. It is something inside you; not dependent upon any condition or set of circumstances outside you. You can decide for peace right now and dedicate your life to expressing it.

And God said unto Moses, 'I AM THAT I AM' and he said, 'Thus shalt thou say unto the children of Israel, I AM hath sent me unto you'
– Exodus 3:14.

If you aren't in the moment, you are either looking forward to uncertainty, or back to pain and regret
- Jim Carrey, *60 Minutes*, November 21, 2004.

When presented with inevitable challenges in life, you can go through changes knowing that an eternal peace exists in your being. That knowledge gives you a sense of security as you grow into the life you want. Your growth will then arise from who you really are, not because you need to prove your worth. As you realize your spiritual heritage and infinite riches now, you connect to possibilities in your life and loosen restrictions.

Your connection to 'I Am,' to your Higher Self, expands you. With that awareness, you also realize that the surface divisions of self and others, rich or poor, white or black, male or female are socially constructed, as underneath we are all one.

The Spirit that gives consciousness to you is also present in all. You can appreciate the cultural, racial, gender and linguistic differences between people; yet you *also* recognize that humanity is essentially united in Spirit.

'I Am' awareness also lets you be totally immersed in your activity, with your mind being totally present in what you are doing. Often you can allow your life to run on auto-pilot, which is essential for routine daily tasks, yet meaningful connection in your life demands your presence, not your absence.

When you're talking to your partner, a friend, your children, or your mother or father, how involved are you in the conversation? You can't pretend to be listening because they'll know.

With ongoing neglect, that relationship can suffer and weaken. Even if this has happened, you can still change it. You can exercise your presence in conversations, by active listening and your full presence.

As you open to others, they will also open up to you and in time, your relationship can be restored.

How to know if You Are Living from 'I Am'

Finally, what I really want is to be happy in this moment, where the magic and miracles happen. Stay in the moment and all gifts are added as you breathe and take inspired action
– **Joe Vitale**

'I Am' awareness is activating your connection to Spirit. You can know if you're living in 'I Am,' by asking a simple question: *'Where do I spend most of my time – in the past, future or present?'*

If you are anywhere but the present, then you need to reconnect to your Spiritual Core. Just as with exercise, you get better with routine and training, the same holds true for your Consciousness. If you already live most of your life in the present, then you already have a healthy connection to Spirit.

Another way to tell if you are connected to your Spirit centre is by asking yourself: *'Am I experiencing joy right now?'* Or are you waiting for something to happen? Do you say to yourself: 'Well, I'll be happy after I find a soul-mate, have a certain job, or have more money?'

While you need to know what you want for the future, still you need to experience joy, peace and happiness now through your connection with Spirit. When you start with joy, peace and happiness, then you plant those qualities as seeds. In time as a tree grows its fruits will be sweetened by those qualities. Spirit creates life: Spirit exists before a seed or an embryo takes form. Even when the body dies according to spiritual traditions the Spirit continues.

When you are connected to Spirit, you are happy now and unconcerned with the past or future. So start to live in the present, which is where all miracles happen. The past is gone and future is yet to be but in this moment now is when your life unfolds. Learn to live with full presence, being truly alive.

How to Activate 'I Am'

You Have Already Arrived. Spirit or 'I Am' is already present; you only need to become aware. You can activate Spirit or 'I Am' in a few different ways. You want to experience joy, peace and contentment first and this will align you to manifest abundance in all aspects of your life.

The word Spirit is derived from Latin *spirare*, 'to breathe.' Breathing is connected to our breath, yet breath also has deeper significance that is life itself. As long as you breathe, you are alive, when you take your last breath, then you expire.

'Expire' comes from Latin *expirare*, literally meaning 'to breathe out your last.' This is why your breath is directly connected to Spirit and when you pay attention to breath you awaken to Spirit.

So as breath is life, Spirit is life, the Consciousness that witnesses all life events. Often Spirit has been thought of as transcendental, yet we want you to recognize Spirit as Joyful and Creative in the here and now.

Spirit is part of your life, allowing you to delight in simple pleasures and have fun. So Spirit lightens your load and gives you optimism in all that you do.

How to Activate Spirit

1. Work with Angel Jophiel

Whether we are filled with joy or grief, our angels are close to us, speaking to our hearts of God's love
– **Eileen Elias Freeman**, *The Angels' Little Instruction Book.*

You might enjoy working with angels. Even if you haven't worked with angels before, this can be a good way to start and to allow for some 'magic' in your life.

The main angel for Spirit is Jophiel, Hebrew for 'Beauty of God.' Lynn Fischer in *Angels of Love and Light* describes Jophiel as the angel of 'illumination,' archangel of paradise, and the patron of artists.

The qualities associated with Jophiel show that this angel accurately personifies different aspects of Spirit. Jophiel can function as a visual image of Spirit for those who find this comforting. Here are some common qualities Fisher associates with Jophiel:

- Stirs feeling for spiritual things.
- Teaches about the power of spiritual illumination.
- Helps in assimilating information, including studying and passing tests.
- Offers knowledge, humility and broadmindedness.
- Provides ethical guidance.
- A sense of responsibility such as making our planet a better place.
- Appreciation of beauty that surrounds you.
- Inspiration for artistic and intellectual thought.

119

Jophiel is depicted both as a male or female, showing that Spirit is beyond gender. Through visualization and asking help of this angel, you can find a deep connection to Spirit.

Affirmation
'Jophiel, I ask for your blessings, guidance and presence in my life.'

2. Activate Spirit through Authenticity

It seems to me that people look at God in the wrong way. They think that God is there to serve them, but it's the other way around – **Nick Cave** (Observer, May 1998)

When you work with Spirit, you need an authentic relationship because the Universe and you are co-creators. You're not doing it alone. Spirit is working with you as a guide and loving friend. This means that you are willing to listen to Spirit.

When you look at your own life, you can observe that during your childhood your development was from dependence to independence. As an adult, your growth comes from interdependence, from building and maintaining relationships. Co-creation means visualizing the Spirit as a partner in your personal development, who looks after your best interest and Spirit is also concerned for those around you.

A personal relationship with Spirit is essential for manifesting the best in your life. Just as in any close relationship you learn to listen and to share your dreams. This is an ongoing process of ever deepening understanding, respect and love.

The Universe can serve you but is not your servant. If you treat the Universe as a servant, then through your arrogance you have created a hierarchy. That separation does not allow for you to receive guidance from the Universe, so your communication becomes one-sided based on a list of your wants without responsibilities or a higher purpose.

Only through authentic relationship with the Universe can you experience companionship and infinite possibilities because you are open to receive. You need to know what you want but you also need to know what the Universe asks of you. When you connect to something bigger than you, this can give your life direction, purpose and meaning as you expand from limited thinking to greater awareness.

When you are truly open, then you can manifest your best and you continually grow as the Universe can guide your growth. Sincerity is essential for developing an authentic relationship with Spirit.

What Does An Authentic Bond With Spirit Look Like?

An authentic relationship with Spirit/Universe can translate into knowing that this Higher Power exists now and forever. Spirit has designed you with unique gifts and talents to enable you to fulfill your Life Purpose and to be joyously creative in your life. When you were born, Spirit was there, joyous with your birth and offering wonder, peace and happiness on your personal journey.

Spirit is like a true and loving friend, who encourages, supports and leads you through the dark times of fear, despair and doubt. Spirit is also with you to share times of great joy and success. Spirit desires that you live a life of wellness, purpose, and abundance.

Authentic Communication

Just as with any relationship, good communication is also essential with Spirit, based on being fully present and developing that presence in your daily life. Through meditation, prayer and present moment awareness, the voice of Spirit becomes easier to discern under the chatter of your mind and the noise of the world.

Spirit already knows of the goings on at the very depths of your soul. When you meditate or pray it is not to inform Spirit of your desires but to experience the presence of peace in your life. The communication is about developing a relationship based on unconditional love.

You love because you are inspired to love, not because Spirit will always give in to your demands. If your love were only based on getting, then your love stops being authentic. Instead focus on creating space for Spirit in your life and allow that presence to inspire you. So before you start any project in your life, first know peace from direct, personal communication with Spirit.

As you trust Spirit, you also gain confidence that the Universe will provide for your needs. This can increase the flow of synchronicity in your life. So as you become aware of your deeper inspirations, the right people, events and experiences start to effortlessly find expression in your life.

3. Activate Spirit with Meditation

Meditation allows us to access the world of spirit through stillness
– **Wayne Dyer.**

Dr. Herbert Benson, Associate Professor at Harvard Medical School and founder of Mind Body Medical Institute, has described in *The Relaxation Response* the numerous benefits of meditation or relaxation. They include easing anxiety, pain and distress, relieving fatigue, and increasing hope. Even blood pressure, sleep, mood and overall health improved. Meditation causes many of these changes through releasing hormones and neurotransmitters.

Dr. Benson shows that normally the mind and body are conditioned by the 'Fight-or-Flight' Response, where you fearfully either prepare to do battle or to run from threats. That tension in mind and body drains you. But, when you engage in meditation and learn to relax, you let go of all tensions, and experience healing and rejuvenation from the largest muscles to the tiniest cells.

Through visualization, you can learn to direct healing energy wherever you need it. The best part of meditation is that it is available to you any time, at no cost and you can administer it without side effects.

How to Connect with Spirit through Meditation

Through realization of Self, you dwell within the home of Spirit
– **Guru Nanak** (Guru Granth Sahib, 57-17)

You can connect to Spirit by developing an inner focus, where you allow your mind to relax, slow down and become quiet.

You need to focus on your breathing as it becomes deeper, your heart rate slows down, and your awareness is focused on the present moment.

If you are new to meditation or think that it is difficult, just know that when you daydream; when you are absorbed in a book, movie, or in music you experience a state of meditation.

Whenever attention becomes focused, then you enter meditation. Focusing on breath may take some time because your mind may have a lot of chatter. That's okay; it's normal. Now through meditation you can relax, let go and just observe. Let whatever happens, happen.

Breath Meditation:

1. Your breath is most connected to Sprit. So here is a Breath Meditation: Find a quiet place and get into a comfy position with the back straight. You can sit on the ground cross-legged or sit in a chair with feet on the floor.
2. Gently close your eyes and take a deep breath in
3. Observe your in-breath as cool and your out-breath as warm. As you take a few more deep breaths, let your breathing become deep and rhythmic.
4. On the next inhalation whisper 'I Am' and when you exhale also repeat 'I Am.' Now continue to say 'I Am' with each breath you take.
5. Allow thoughts to arise and gently bring your awareness to your breath and 'I Am' awareness.
6. Continue the meditation for 10 to 15 minutes your first week, adding 5 minutes each week, until you can meditate relatively easily for 30 minutes. If you need to move around, you can do so, just bring your awareness to breath and 'I Am.'

This practice is naturally awareness and whatever thoughts, emotions and sensations arise fully accept them. Acknowledge them and gently bring your awareness back to breath and the present moment awareness of 'I Am.'

4. Activate Spirit through Archetypes

The concept of the archetype ... indicates the existence of definite forms in the psyche which seem to be present always and everywhere
– Carl Jung.

What Is An Archetype?

An Archetype is a universal pattern or symbol that your Spirit knows. Since a relationship with a mere concept is remote, you need to work with familiar images, such as: Child, Self, Father, Mother, Warrior and Mother Earth.

How Do You Work With An Archetype?

You want to develop an emotional bond with the archetype. For example, when you learn about the Child, you want to make this image emotionally charged for you by drawing upon your own experiences with children. This can be your own children, children around you, or memories of your own childhood. Try to look at experiences from a Child's sense of wonder. Archetypal images have the power to transform you from your emotional attachment to them.

The Self Archetype

We do not attract what we want, but what we are
– James Allen.

Most of us are anxious to improve our circumstances, but are unwilling to improve ourselves—and we therefore remain bound
– James Allen.

The Self represents you as a whole; it represents your greatest potential. The Self goes beyond a contracted self-image and allows you to be complete and live up to your true potential. What you envision to become in all aspects of your life, when you want to balance and integrate your life, then you are developing Self.

Your Self expresses what has personal meaning for you. There is no right or wrong answer here. We all want different things. Knowing Self is uncovering what you truly want out of life.

What will make life meaningful for you? Through the process of Self-development you become whole and powerful. You are determined to be your very best and to do your very best. As Spirit expands your vision to a universal perspective, you can go beyond the limits of prejudices and biases.

The divisions of race, class and nationality yield to a greater unity and oneness. Through Self you also recognize the inner beauty of other people. You will find that you are non-judgmental because as you accept yourself, you also accept those around you.

Through awareness of Self you recognize the wealth of your own inner qualities and how they can contribute to the world. The Self asks you to be fully you, and not to settle for anything less. As you are part of something greater than you, you can expand beyond any limits. The Self is an expanded you and the Spirit is the part of Universe contained in an individual.

The narrative of the life of Jesus from birth, crucifixion to the resurrection parallels the growth of Self. Just as does the life of other teachers: Moses, Buddha, Muhammad, Nanak and Krishna. These teachers offer guidance for personal growth and you can learn from their example. During their early life, we find the interplay of the Divine and the Child in them until later in their life you can locate the totality of Self.

The Child Archetype

I tell you the truth, unless you change and become like little children, you will never enter the kingdom of heaven
– **Jesus** (Matthew 18:3)

Grown men may learn from very little children, for the hearts of little children are pure
– **Black Elk** (The Sacred Pipe*)*

Eternity is a child playing, playing checkers; the kingdom belongs to a child
– **Heraclitus**.

There's no point in being grown-up if you can't be childish sometimes
– **Doctor Who** ('Robot' episode)

The Spirit is about play, creativity, imagination, wonder and innocence, as expressed by the Child or in religious figures the Divine Child. The longing for a return to innocence shown by the Child is the desire to restore a real connection with Spirit. Children are imaginative and unfettered by rigid thinking. Adults can often feel a longing to reconnect to childhood joy and playfulness. This is why you can find the Child archetype in familiar animated characters, including:

- Calvin from *Calvin and Hobbes*, whose imagination creates hilarious adventures with Hobbes, his stuffed tiger.
- Linus van Pelt, from *Peanuts* comic strip, is unusually smart often quoting the Gospels but he is still a child who carries his blue blanket with him.
- Lisa Simpson from *The Simpsons*, is very intelligent. She plays the sax, has chosen to become a vegetarian, and supports many progressive causes.

The Child calls you to balance being a grown-up, with the joy and innocence of being child-like. Adults can forget how to have fun in life because they get too busy being serious. The Child allows you to step outside your negative vibe and feel a sense of wonder for tomorrow, no matter what your age. For those who have children, you know they break up the seriousness of life through play, imagination and just plain fun. When you allow yourself to be playful, your creativity is boosted. Brainstorming exercises are essentially playfulness with ideas. That combined with a sense of wonder can create magic in your life where you can envision your dreams and see or feel them coming true.

As you start to reconnect to the Child inside you, you'll often remember your own childhood: The things you enjoyed, what fascinated or amused you, and what made you curious. Take a moment to remember when you were a child. If you could play, imagine and have fun as a child again, would that balance out your life?

The exploration of the Child archetype is all about joy. If in case this brings up uncomfortable memories for you, we recommend that you work with a caring professional who can guide you through the experience.

How Do You Reconnect To Your Own Child?

When you look at children or remember yourself as a child, you remember how simple life was back then.

How much joy you experienced jumping in puddles, riding a bike, or going to the beach. In your life, are you just keeping on top of tasks? Have you forgotten about experiencing joy?

You can take time out of your busy day to spend on activities that give you joy – the kind of joy that you experienced as a child.

- As an adult, you might have let work take over your life. You can change that by starting to play again – play with kids, pets, or play sports with your friends.
- Learn to be creative again. Do you want to paint, bake, sing, play music, dance, go for a ride, or take a trip? Well, do what you want for the sheer fun!
- Play with old toys or games, or try new ones that appeal to you – this includes play-doh, soap bubbles, a kite, a remote control car, dominoes, board games, marbles, hop-scotch, jumping rope or playing ball.
- Read a joke book and exercise humour in your life, approach situations with a cheerful attitude
- Have fun with the weather: Jump in puddles, walk in the rain, go for a bike ride, jump on leaves, or make snow angels
- Take up childhood hobbies. What did you collect in your childhood? Comic books? Action figures? Sports cars? Doll houses? Were you fascinated by animals? Sports stars? Heroes? Movie stars?
- Daydream again
- Take time to relax and take naps

Daydreams and/or imagination are essential for Visualization. So getting in touch with your Child has practical benefits. Reconnecting to your Sprit through the Child archetype is full of joy, play and imagination. Those qualities are essential for making any venture in life happy and exciting.

You can also start to dream, realize what you care about, and what you need to feel good. The Spirit as Your Inner Child can help you find joy, creativity and wonder.

Allowing Sprit To Grant Your Wishes

The Child has trust in adults around him or her. In the same way you can have trust in the Universe. Children will ask for what they want, without reservation. You can also do the same through this exercise:

1. If you could ask Spirit three wishes, what would they be? Write down the answers as they come to your mind. Next place a number 1, 2 and 3 next to each answer according to greatest to least priority that you give to each wish.
2. Now ask Spirit for guidance, help and direction to achieve your #1 wish on your list.
3. Be open for Spirit to grant your #2 or #3 wish if those are most suitable to your growth.
4. Let Spirit also know that you are open to receive any of your wishes or something better.
5. Allow Spirit to work with you and have joy because of this co-creative partnership.
6. Always thank the Universe for all that it has given you.
7. Trust the Universe and allow all to manifest in Divine time.

2. Activate Spirit through Being Centered

Be still and know that I am God (Psalm 46:10)

When you look at or imagine a wheel in movement where is the greatest movement? Is it on the outside where the rim is located or inside where the hub is located? Notice that the centre is still but the outside quickly rotates.

Likewise, at the core of your Being you are centred regardless of surface movement. The disturbances are only on the outside but inside you is peace.

When you throw a stone into water, you have ripples form on the surface but underneath the water is still.

In the same way, on the surface you might perceive disturbance but underneath is a gentle flow. When you get back to the centre, then you connect to the peace that is always within you.

Why Do You Need Centering?

You need to start from peace when you begin any endeavour. When you start with peace, you plant peace as your future; for as you sow, so you reap. So if you have sown anxiety, then you cannot expect a harvest of peace.

You need to start to sow peace now in your Spirit. Here is a Centering Prayer to help you get started:

What Is Centering Prayer?

Father Thomas Keating, a Trappist monk and priest, explains Centering Prayer as 'two friends sitting in silence, being in each other's presence.' In this type of prayer you move beyond images, emotions and thoughts.

Centering Prayer is more a receptive, silent meditation unlike traditional forms of prayer through words. Centering Prayer is focused on a loving relationship and uses words only as an aid. You let yourself open up to direct experience of God's presence in stillness and peace.

Over time with Centering Prayer you let go of your false Self-Worth and return to your True Self. You start to express your Self in your daily life. The process is ongoing as you continue to develop a deeper relationship with Spirit.

God's main language is silence, and through Prayer you can sit comfortably with silence. With Centering Prayer you leave all intentions behind, such as, to have no thoughts, to feel peaceful, or to achieve a spiritual experience. You just effortlessly allow experience to manifest.

In the Roman Catholic tradition Contemplative Prayer is considered to be a gift of God in which the heart, mind and being are opened to God, who is beyond thoughts, words, and emotions. A similar tradition to Contemplative Prayer is found in many other spiritual traditions, including Repetition of the Name or *Nam Japna* in Sikhism, Remembrance or *Dhikr* in Sufism, chanting of *Mantra* such as OM by Hindus and Buddhists, and the silence of the Quakers. Almost all traditions have something similar to this form of quiet meditation

How to Do It

You set aside 15 to 20 minutes daily for this prayer where you open yourself up to and rest in Spirit's Presence. You can use a quiet timer to help you keep track of the time.

1. Choose a word such as love, peace or silence as your intention to open up to God's presence.
2. Sit comfortably and with eyes closed, relax, and silently introduce the sacred word.
3. When thoughts arise, gently return to your word.
4. At the end of the prayer period, stay silent with eyes closed for a few minutes. Then slowly open your eyes and rub your hands together to return feeling to your body.

3. Activate Spirit through Use of Symbols

Symbols are the form that an archetype takes in your daily life. The symbol gives concrete form to an abstract idea contained in an archetype. Symbols make visible your intention through an outside object such as a sculpture, drawing or shape.

When you use symbols wisely you can activate powerful states of being that allow your intentions to manifest in your life.

By consciously bringing symbols into your personal space, you prove to yourself that through intention you can create a new environment around you. You also take steps to improve your life and integrate your learning into your life. For example, you will learn to create a space for meditation, which can include symbols that you personally find meaningful.

Those of you, who have worked with the Law of Attraction, have already worked with this powerful tool through the use of a Vision Board. Through the Vision Board, you were able to make your intentions concrete, visible and experiential. You can do the same for all aspects of your life, including working with Spirit.

Through symbols you are activating powerful mental images and connecting the inner and outer world into a unified field of intention.

Your chosen symbols will reflect what you most desire to manifest in your life. You might want Wholeness, Oneness or Centeredness for Spirit and you can create or find a symbol to express this intention.

You can add your chosen symbol to your personal space, visualize it in an exercise or even wear it.

How Do Symbols Activate Spirit?

Symbols can function on different aspects of Spirit and through them you can activate the particular area where you want to focus and grow. Here are common goals where you can use symbols:

1. *Wholeness/Oneness/Unity*: This is based on the desire to have balance and harmony in your life. You want to see the bigger picture and find a greater purpose and meaning in your life.

2. *Centering/Self-growth*: You want to find a deeper understanding of Self and live your life with greater authenticity. You are interested in integrating aspects of your being.

3. *Joy/Peace*: You want to find lasting joy and peace in your life that comes from an inner security, which is independent of anything or anyone outside. With that security you can find happiness in all areas of your life.

1. Symbols of Wholeness/Oneness/Unity

Circle – Perfection, Wholeness, Completeness

The power of the world always works in circles, and everything tries to be round. In the old days when we were a strong and happy people, all our power came to us from the sacred hoop of the nation, and so long as the hoop was unbroken the people flourished
- Black Elk (Black Elk Speaks)

Circle

The circle is perhaps the most natural, profound and common symbol in existence. The heavenly stars, planets and moons are shaped as circles. The seasons, elements, and the life cycle of a person are seen as a circle. While a line represents a hierarchy, the circle represents unity, equality and oneness between all members. A circle also represents infinity, eternity and wholeness because it has no beginning or end.

Other meaningfully significant symbols or objects that are circular include: Stonehenge, Ouroboros, Crop Circles, and the Halo around the head of saints in paintings.

Mandalas and Labyrinths are an elaboration of the basic circle and represent the journey to the centre. Among American Native traditions the circle is present in Sacred Hoops and Medicine Wheel.

Circles are one of the earliest shapes found in Prehistoric art found on the walls of prehistoric caves and rock faces. In astrology, the circle represents Spirit, who you really are, as opposed to outer personality, how others see you.

The circle is used as symbol for Spirit while Earth is represented by four quarters (+) or a square. The circle due to its cyclical nature is connected to the goddess and female energies among contemporary pagans. It is also connected to cycles: Seasons, rotation of the Earth, movement of stars, and the movement of planet around orbits. Animals and Plants are aware of these cycles more so than are humans.

They instinctively respond to climatic changes, as shown in the migration of birds, hibernation of bears in winter, or the dormancy of plants. In many traditions, women are traditionally thought to be more in touch with cycles; experiencing menstruation, childbirth, and menopause.

This is why the feminine principle is often associated with nature and earth. The problem has arisen when human civilization has tried to dominate both nature and the earth; the association had also led to the lowering of the status of women.

The trend is changing to an egalitarian understanding as we become increasingly aware of inequalities in society and develop a greater respect for the environment as Mother Earth.

The circle is the perfect symbol for equality, unity and oneness as it represents relationships in a non-hierarchical pattern within a sphere instead of a line, where each individual is part of a greater whole and united with each other. This is different than the linear way of thinking responsible for creating many of our current hierarchies.

When we think of relationships in terms of the circle, we are comprehending their Spiritual Wholeness, where Spirit and Earth while different are essentially united, male and female are unique yet equal, and racial and cultural differences while visible still allow us share a harmonious circle of shared human experiences.

In mystical traditions, circle is symbol of God and infinity. It is a symbol of heaven and everything spiritual. In magical traditions, circles are considered protection. This is why Wiccan rites often begin with drawing a circle. In Feng Shui, the circle stands for heaven (*yin*). Round-shaped objects such as bowls, unlock creative and spiritual energies with their openness.

The circle has many interesting spiritual associations: The halo is a zone of light behind the head of a holy figure, used for Christ, Mary, and saints in Christian art.

Spirit Circle Visualization Exercise

1. Gently close your eyes.
2. Take a deep in-breath to the count of 1, 2 and 3 – breathing in vital energy
3. Breathe-out 1, 2 and 3 – releasing all tension.
4. Breathe in again 1, 2 and 3.
5. Breathe out 1, 2 and 3.
6. Now continue to breathe deeply and rhythmically allowing your breath to easily fall-in and fall-out.
7. Sit comfortably with a feeling of peace and quiet.
8. Now picture or feel a bright golden circle in your mind and make its shape and colour clear.
9. Next, feel that you are part of it. As the circle is whole, complete and infinite, so are you.
10. Imagine the golden circle in the shape of a spherical ball is filled with light and is just above your head.
11. The circle is now above your head.
12. If the mind wanders, as it often will, then wait a moment or two and guide it gently back.
13. Chant or intone the words: 'I AM' and feel the presence of Spirit.
14. Take a deep inhalation 1, 2, 3.
15. Again intone: 'I AM' and meditate on the presence of Spirit for a few minutes.

16. As you close this exercise, know that the circle represents 'I Am' conscious within.
17. Now gently open your eyes and bring 'I Am' Awareness to your daily life through your presence in each moment, in all your activities.

The Sky/Heavens

The sky represents infinity, immortality and order. A painting of clear blue sky or with soft billowy clouds can bring the vastness of the heavens into your life.

Other Symbols of Wholeness/Oneness/Unity: Om or Aum, Ik Onkar, Wheels, Ankh, Celtic Cross, Infinity Symbol, Shiva, Spiral, Vishnu, Zen Circle, God/Goddess.

Oneness/Unity/Wholeness Exercise

For this exercise we want you to select a symbol that represents Oneness/Unity/Wholeness either from those listed in the previous section. Or you can take any other symbol that you know expresses these qualities.

Now, work with your chosen symbol as follows:

• Relax, take a few deep breaths and close your eyes.
• Imagine or visualize your desired symbol for 'Oneness/Unity/Wholeness.'
• Allow the symbol to become clear in your mind.
• Now meditate on how this symbol expresses Oneness/Unity/Wholeness. What shape and colour is the symbol? What feeling or meaning do you associate with it?
• Allow your mind to settle on this symbol and for the next few minutes focus your mind on it. If other thoughts arise, label

them as thought, emotion, restlessness, etc. Then let it go, bringing your focus back to your symbol.
- Once again let it become clear in your mind.
- After a few minutes have passed, imagine or visualize the symbol pulsating with energy and say three times: 'I Am One, United, Whole' and with each repetition feel these words in your whole being.
- Allow yourself to relax in the presence of the Oneness, Unity and Wholeness.
- When you're ready open your eyes, look all around you and bring Oneness/Unity/Wholeness into your daily life.

When you feel One/Whole/United, then your energies are integrated. You are one in all aspects of your being: Mind, Body and Spirit. All five elements of Spirit, Air, Fire, Water and Earth are balanced and what they represent is also activated in your life.

2. Symbols for Centering/Self-growth

Circled Dot

This is a circle with a point at its centre representing the Spiritual Centre that exists in every individual linking him or her to the source of creativity. From this centre, you can become a co-creator of your world.

Many of the symbols associated with Centering and Self-growth have this basic symbolism at their root of an outer circle with an inner centre including: Mandalas, rose windows and labyrinths.

Mandala – For Positive Changes in Your Life

A page from a journal of modern experimental physics will be as mysterious to the uninitiated as a Tibetan mandala. Both are records of enquiries into the nature of the universe - Fritjof Capra, *The Tao of Physics*, 1975.

In Sanskrit, Mandala means 'Sacred Circle.' It is essentially a design for centering yourself.

It is a beautiful example of 'squaring the circle' with merging of Spirit energy represented by a circle with the energy of the Earth represented by the square.

The mandala is often illustrated as a palace with four entrances to the centre representing Earth energy returning to Spirit.

How to Make Your Own Mandala:

You can make a mandala simply by drawing a circle and then creating an image within it. A self-created mandala reflects your Inner Self at the time you draw it along with your potential for growth.

Making a mandala is similar to meditating, whether you paint, draw, or design your image on a computer.

You can even design one based on mathematical fractals, a shape that can divide into halves.

Cathy A. Malchiodi, Art Therapist, has offered practical guidelines for creating a mandala on her website: http://www.cathymalchiodi.com as adapted below:

Material You Need:

1. Several sheets of 12' x 12' white paper.
2. Oil pastel crayons, coloured chalks or plain crayons.
3. A round plate (about 10' in diameter) to trace a circle or you can use a compass.
4. A graphite pencil to sketch in any preliminary designs
5. A ruler for making straight lines.

How to draw a mandala:

- On the white paper in pencil trace a plate.
- With your drawing materials, fill in the circle with any colours, lines and shapes you want.
- Shapes can mean different things, so use shapes that express the energy you wish:
  - o Circle – Spirit
  - o Upward Triangle – Desire to manifest more Spirit in your life
  - o Downward Triangle – Desire to manifest more Earth/Material things in your life
  - o Square – Earth
  - o Pentacle or Star – Human Being, Integration of Spirit and Earth
- You can start at the centre or the edges of the circle.
- You can divide up the space in the circle in some way.

- You may want to create a pattern or fill the space with a variety of shapes and color.
- Feel free to go outside the circle if you wish.
- Continue to add to your drawing until you are happy.

Carl Jung referred to mandalas as 'cryptograms,' coded messages from your inner self. The mandala is a symbol of the Self in its essential wholeness. As you look at your own mandala what do you sense about it. In this exercise, you intentionally added shapes that accorded with your desires, what energy did you want to increase or manifest in your life?

Cultures around the world have often used mandala patterns in their sacred and healing art. Examples include cathedral rose windows, labyrinths, and Navajo and Tibetan sand paintings. Native Americans Shamans had worked with healing power within the circle.

Much of the symbolic geometry of Native American art and ritual predominantly figures a balance of cycles expressed in a circle along with its division into the four directions: North, South, East and West. The Medicine Wheel is a good example of this idea.

The Rose Window seen in Gothic cathedrals is a circular window with a design that resembles flower petals. The finest examples are found in French Chartres Cathedral and Notre Dame Cathedral.

Labyrinth

Another interesting design common in the West is the Labyrinth, which are pathways leading to the centre and back out by retracing your steps. Unlike mazes, where you can get lost or trapped a labyrinth is a clear journey to the centre with no obstacles.

It is a diagram of your way to your spiritual centre and then a return to the world. As you walk a labyrinth in real life or through visualization, you can leave the cares of the world and enter a peaceful, secure space.

Those who are more devout, value the labyrinth as a pilgrimage through which you can discover something about yourself and God.

When you walk a labyrinth, the destination is less important than the journey itself. You can forget this truth in the fast-pace of life. Or when you really want something, you become so caught up in getting it that you forget to be joyous NOW.

The labyrinth is a great way for you to come back to reality, and recognize that your journey needs to be fun – the destination will take care of itself. 'The Man in The Maze' is a variation of the labyrinth by Natives in Mexico and the Southwest United States.

How Do You Walk A Labyrinth?

First visit labyrinthlocator.com online to locate a labyrinth near you. To walk the labyrinth, let Spirit guide you along the way. Depending on the setting, you can:

- Maintain silence for your reflection and for others.
- You can focus your thoughts on each step.
- Notice your breathing.
- Note how the path twists and turns but eventually you will come to the centre as in life.
- Enter with a receptive, joyous attitude.
- Walk at your own pace and allow others to move around you.
- After your walk, stay quietly at the centre.
- Make your journey back when you sense it is time to return.
- After note how it felt going to the centre and then returning.

Going to the centre is connecting to Spirit and going back out to the world is connecting with Earth.

Labyrinth Visualization Exercise

Besides visiting a labyrinth, you can also visualize or imagine walking one.

1. Clearly visualize the labyrinth. This can be a labyrinth entirely of your own imagination, one that you have visited before, or one you have seen in photos.
2. See or feel that you walk this labyrinth outdoors on a beautiful sunny day. You can hear the birds chirping and a cool, gentle breeze upon your skin.
3. You are at the entrance of the labyrinth and consciously observe silence to centre yourself in the Now.
4. You take off your shoes and socks if you are wearing any and feel the soft grass under your feet. The labyrinth is a safe place where you can walk barefoot.

143

5. Remain silent and peaceful as you enter the labyrinth.
6. Silently walk the path conscious of each step you place on the ground and lift up from the stable earth.
7. You turn at the first turn in the path remaining ever present of each step you take.
8. The turn winds around a bend and you stay present with each step of your journey.
9. You turn another turn in the path and notice that the circle is becoming narrow and you are near the centre.
10. The path continues to gently turn and narrow.
11. With a final turn you find yourself at the very centre. There you find your Spirit waiting for you. You can see the Spirit in a form, as light or just sense the presence. You take a rest on a bench and feel a great sense of peace as you feel the energy of Spirit activated and released into your whole being. Peace, joy and sense of self-worth fill you.
12. You now feel centered and an enthusiasm spreads throughout your body and you feel the need to journey back into the world with your energy and awareness.
13. You make the journey back taking the direct route out from the centre and find that your perception of the world is changed. You feel a sense of wonder, enthusiasm and you are thankful for the gift of life.
14. As you return to the world, you connect with the rhythms of Earth while staying centered to Spirit or Self within.

Other Symbols for Centering/Self-growth: Bodhi Tree, Feather, Tree, White Lotus, The Holy Grail, Child, Cosmic Man, Mountain, Rocks, Bamboo, Chalice, Diamonds, Gazelle, Jesus, Muhammad, Moses, Buddha, Nanak, Saints, Sparrow, Gandhi, Mahavira, Solomon, Zoroaster, Confucius, Lao Tzu

Centering/Self-growth Exercise

For this exercise we want you to select a symbol that represents Centering/Self-growth either from those listed in the section above. Or you can take any other symbol that you know about which conveys the idea of 'Centering/Self-growth.' Try to select a symbol you can fill with personal meaning, maybe from your faith such as the founder – Jesus, Buddha, Muhammad or Moses, spiritual understanding, or based on your strong inclinations. Or if you are unsure, choose a symbol and give it personal meaning. Now work with your chosen symbol as follows:

- Relax, take a few deep breaths, and close your eyes.
- See or feel your symbol for 'Centering/Self-growth.'
- Take some time for it to become clear in your mind.
- Now meditate on how this symbol expresses Centering/Self-growth for you. What shape or colour is it? Is it a person? What feelings or meaning do you associate with it?
- Allow your mind to settle on this symbol and for the next few minutes focus your mind it. If other thoughts arise, label them as: thought, emotion, restlessness or any other suitable label. Then let the thought go, bringing your focus back to your symbol.
- Once again let it become clear in your mind.
- After a few minutes have passed, imagine or visualize the symbol pulsating as your emotional connection to it grows, then say: 'I Am Centered Within' three times and each time you feel the words resonate in your whole being. Hold these feelings for a few moments, letting the emotional meaning of the symbol become real for you. Then consider how this symbol can assist you in your own growth.
- Allow yourself to relax in the presence of the aspect of Spirit as Centering/Self-growth.
- When you are ready open your eyes and go into life with a sense of being centered and growing in ever-expanding ways.

3. Symbols for Joy/Peace/Innocence/Hope

Angel – Joy, Peace, Help

Angels, from Latin 'messenger', are perfect symbols for joy, beauty and innocence of Spirit. They express dignity, glory, help

145

and revelation. You can use angel sculptures or pictures to ask for protection and guidance.

Bell – Joy, Freedom

The bell is used as musical instrument, ritual object, and as a way to enter and stop meditation. Bells are a symbol of joy and freedom as is the American Liberty Bell. You can even use it to welcome friends even angels. Due to its roundish shape, the bell also represents Spirit.

Butterfly – Joy, Creativity, Transformation

Butterflies function as a symbol of joy at Spirit and also transformation at the Water Element.

Candle – Hope, Illumination, Peace

The candle offers hope and peace as a symbol of light in dark times. It is a symbol of spiritual light, illumination and salvation. They are part of religious rituals.

Dove – Peace, Forgiveness

In ancient Greek myth the dove was the bird of Athena, which represented the renewal of life. In the Genesis 8:11, the dove released by Noah returned with an olive branch signifying the end of the Flood. Since then the dove has become a symbol of deliverance and forgiveness. The olive branch and the dove are both symbols of peace. In Christianity, the dove is a symbol of the soul and represents the Holy Spirit. It signifies peacefulness, purity and gentleness.

Hummingbird – Joy, Sweetness

The small and elusive hummingbird is a perfect symbol for optimism, joy and sweetness. They can hover in mid-air, an ability that reminds us to stay in the moment. With their long beaks, they are quickly able to get to sweet nectar.

Gardens – Joy, Happiness

The garden is a safe and protective earthly paradise. Happiness, purity and mystical ecstasy are considered aspects of a garden. Spending time in a garden can rejuvenate the Spirit and offers delight to the senses.

Unicorn – Healing, Purity, Strength

A fabled creature is a horse with a spiralled horn. It is associated with healing, purity and moral strength.

Other Symbols for Joy/Peace/Innocence/Hope: Fairies, Bees, Cherub, Child, Conch Shell, Crane, Daisies, Dragonfly, Krishna, Peace Symbol, Daffodils, Elf, Gladiolas, Gnome, Lamp, Light, Lilies, Pony.

Joy/Peace/Innocence/Hope Exercise

For this exercise we want you to select a symbol that represents Joy/Peace/Innocence/Hope either from symbols noted in the section above. Or you can take any other symbol that offers these qualities to you. Try to select a symbol that connects to happy memories or associations. This can be a symbol connected to your childhood, to your most memorable holiday, to nature, to something funny, or to your loving relationships. Choose whatever makes you feel happy and light. Now work with your chosen symbol as follows:

- Relax, take a few deep breaths and close your eyes.
- Imagine/visualize a symbol of 'Joy/Peace/Innocence/Hope.'
- Take some time for the symbol to become clear in your mind.
- After your symbol is clear, now meditate on how this symbol expresses Joy/Peace/Innocence/Hope for you. What shape or colour is the symbol? How does the symbol make you feel happy? Would feeling more joyous allow you to have more enthusiasm in your life?
- Allow your mind to settle on this symbol and for the next few minutes focus your mind on this symbol. If others thoughts arise, label them as: thought, emotion, restlessness or any

other suitable label. Then let the thought go, bringing your focus back to your symbol.

- Once again let it become clear in your mind.
- After a few minutes have passed, see or feel the symbol pulsating as your own happiness grows, then say: 'I Am connected to Joy/Peace/Innocence/Hope' three times and each time you say it allow yourself to feel waves of happiness. Hold these feelings for a few moments, letting the joy of symbol make you feel lighter. If suitable, reflect on: What gives me most joy in my life? How can I find more ways to express joy?
- Allow yourself to relax in the presence of the aspect of Spirit as Joy/Peace/Innocence/Hope.
- When you're ready open your eyes, look all around you with a sense of Joy and Peace. Decide to make joy and laughter a part of your daily life.

Bring Together Your Spiritual Practice
Create Your Own Meditation Space

As you have practiced growing in Spirit, you may have a space dedicated to the purpose of becoming quiet and centered, a space for meditation. Your meditation space is a reflection of you, of your spiritual needs for quiet, healing and rejuvenation. So create the space according to your vision and needs. Treat the following as only guidelines:

1. First decide upon a location in your home. You want a space that offers:
   a. Quiet
   b. Good lighting ideally with a window and a nice view or at least one that allows sunlight.
   c. Good air circulation
   d. The paint on the walls is soothing. If you do not like the colour of the walls but like the space, then consider repainting the walls.

2. Think about what centeredness, peace, joy and wholeness mean to you.
3. The main purpose(s) of your space will reflect its design:
   a. A sanctuary for meditation, prayer and reflection.
   b. A place of healing and rejuvenation.
   c. Where family or friends can meet for worship.
4. Remove clutter for your chosen space. When you're looking at objects creating clutter, consider do you love, need or want these items? If not, then you can release them. As you let go of items maybe by donating them, you can receive new items suitable for you now.
5. Select items for this space. These items can be based on your meditation on different symbols including those that represent wholeness, centeredness and joy/peace to you. You can get ideas from the symbols and archetypes contained in this chapter. You can decide how many objects you want in this space but look for objects that have personal meaning and are symbolically powerful.
   a. Plants, stones, shells, statues, paintings, bells, sacred texts, wind chimes, and a mat or area rug are worth considering for this space.
6. If your space is limited go with a minimalist look and you can put your desired object on a small table. For this space you can create a space in a section of a room.
7. Add cushions and chairs for sitting and meditation based on your purpose and anticipated need in this space.
8. Making sure your space has the right amount of lighting. Consider adding candles but make sure they are placed safely in candle- holders.
9. Add a small table or altar where you can conveniently place objects.
10. Have a CD player with soothing music or sounds that you enjoy.
11. You can add incense if you find it enjoyable and you can experiment with different types: Sandalwood, Vanilla, Patchouli, Sage, and many more. Or choose a diffuser.

Finishing Exercise
Self as Tree Exercise

- Imagine or visualize a mighty oak, pine or redwood tree. It doesn't matter which one you select just make the idea of this tree clear in your mind.
- Before the tree took form, it was merely a potential in the world of Spirit, containing no form and taking up no space, yet the potential for life and manifestation of an abundant tree were all there. Spirit 'breathed' life into the tree and permitted it to take the form of a seed. This seed was planted in the soil.
- The seed of that tree is planted in the soil of Mind, where pockets of Air allow the root system to develop and grow. Whatever seed you plant will only grow into that tree species: A pine seed grows into a pine, an acorn into an oak, or a redwood seed into redwood. This goes with the saying: 'Whatever you plant, you reap.' So it is important to plant the right seeds in the Mind.
- As the tree sapling often struggles to break through the ground, the tree through its devotion to the sun always grows to the light. The fire element as heat and light energy of the sun feeds, sustains, and nourishes the tree.
- The tree also needs enough Water to grow ideally every few weeks especially in hot weather. For this the tree is dependent on weather produced by the movement of Air currents. Water determines the size of trees and those receiving enough water grow into majestic trees.
- As the tree grows and expands its roots grow deeper into the Earth, so that it can withstand the greatest storms being firmly grounded into the soil.
- What is true for the tree, the same holds true for the Self.
- Keep the growth of the tree in mind as you grow in your own journey. Be patient and know that you grow to the Light.

Chapter Summary

In the Spirit chapter you have learned the importance of starting with Spirit, the 'I Am' Consciousness underlying all your experience. When you start with Spirit, you can activate greater joy, peace and self-growth within you and in all that you do.

Many people have tried to work with the Law of Attraction but they have had mixed success, largely because they had left out a connection with Spirit and without that core to guide their actions, they often became discouraged, felt growing doubt, or even blamed themselves for their 'lack of success.'

We want you to know that true success starts with building a solid inner core, a place within you that allows you to expand and grow into your dreams. You already are Spirit, you just need to experience that Awareness, give it space in your life and you will be rewarded with a co-creative relationship with something that is bigger than you but that is also intimately present in your life.

You have learned many ways to connect to Spirit, knowledge that is life enhancing and powerful, yet to put this into practice is your job. Only you can awaken to what you already are. To activate Spirit, you can work with the Archangel Jophiel, the presiding Angel for Spirit. You can turn to Jophiel in working with Spirit.

We ask that you develop an authentic relationship, where you are a co-creator with Spirit and have a bond based on love, respect and understanding. The Universe knows your needs and is willing to serve you, yet the Universe is not your servant. So you need to approach the Universe with love and practice authentic communication, where an attitude of gratitude is essential for creating growth.

When you are thankful your focus shifts to all the blessings you do have, and from that pure sentiment you can grow. You cannot fake gratitude; it has to be real, sincere. The Universe already knows your desires as your being is centered in the Universe and in Spirit, all you need to do is open up to receive all that Spirit can give you for your growth.

To begin your activation process, start with breath meditation and loosen the sense of control by allowing the energy of Spirit/Universe to work for you.

Yield to peace that is always within you. You will find that doing so will effortlessly drop your regret of the past, and concern for the future. You will start to live your life in the present moment, with 'I Am' awareness. This is where all magic happens in life. When you are present, then you are truly empowered to shift your reality with effective action.

A great aid to activate Spirit is found in powerful archetypal images and in symbols that express your intentions visibly in shapes, diagrams, images, and through your relationship to any spiritual teachers you may have.

The two most powerful archetypes for Spirit are of Self and the Child or Divine Child. The Self is the part of you that grows, expands to a whole you. The Child recaptures the joy, imagination and fun of being child-like in your life. You can find this vividly expressed by the Divine Child as the Buddha, Jesus, Muhammad, Moses, Krishna, Nanak, and other teachers.

The practice of Centering Prayer further allows you to open up to Spirit as part of your daily practice. As with meditation this allows Spirit and you to sit together and develop a relationship where you listen and express your intention for a deeper connection.

Powerful symbols can also inspire you to make your intentions clear and visible. For Spirit symbols offer growth in '*Wholeness, Oneness, Unity.*' The circle is the central image to express this intention. Symbols for '*Centering, Self-growth*' expand on the circle through a circle with a dot at the centre as expressed by different mandala shapes from all over the world. Sometimes this Centering is based on uniting two polarities of yin-yang, male-female. Happiness is activated with symbols expressing '*Joy, Peace, Innocence, Hope.*'

When you light a candle, hear the melodious song of a bird, look at an angel figurine or picture, relate to the Dove as peace, or relax in your garden; then you shift your emotional vibration where joy, peace and hope find expression in you and in your life.

Chart for Spirit Centre

Other Names	Void, Space, God, Higher Self, Divine, Source, Universe, Wholeness, Potentiality, Absolute, Infinity
Characteristics	The Summit/The Pinnacle. Spirit gives Life, Purpose, Mission and Vision
Angel	Jophiel
Element	None, but traditionally associated with Ether, Air from upper heaven, and with Space
Focus	Develop a personal relationship with your Higher Self and the Universe
Location	Starts at top of the head and then travels through all the other Four Elemental Centres of Air, Fire, Water and Earth.
Colours	Gold, Silver and White
Time	All times of the day
Season	All seasons
Represents	The Life Force that breathes Life into Creation
Direction	The Centre
Archetypes	Self, Child and Divine Child
Symbols	Circle, Yin-Yang, Om/Aum, Ik Onkar, Ankh, God/Goddess, Circled Dot, Ouroboros, Mandalas, Labyrinth, Buddha, Jesus, Muhammad, Krishna, Nanak, Moses, Saints, Prophets, Angels, Bell, Dove, Garden, Sky, Light
Gland	Pineal

Spirit to Air

Chapter 6 builds on what you've learned about Spirit. You'll explore how Spirit touches the Air centre with inspiration, and finds expression through thoughts and powerful intentions. The life force is now prepared to be planted in the fertile soil of your mind. You can proceed to the next chapter, or you can linger here to reflect and deepen your practice of Spirit if drawn to do so.

Bibliography for Chapter 5

Bruce, Ann	*Discover True North*
Bradler and Scheiner	*Feng Shui Symbols: A User's Handbook*
Chopra, Deepak and David Simon	*The Seven Spiritual Laws of Yoga*
Cirlot, J.E	*A Dictionary of Symbols*
Regardie, Israel	*The Art of True Healing*
Rinpoche, Thrangu	*Guide to Samantha Meditation*
Thynn, Thynn Dr	*Living Meditation Living Insight*
Tolle, Eckhart	*The Power of Now*
	Stillness Speaks

Chapter **6**

The Air Centre: Formation of Your Character

To think in terms of either pessimism or optimism oversimplifies the truth. The problem is to see reality as it is
– Thich Nhat Hanh, *The Miracle of Mindfulness.*

There is nothing so pitiful as a young cynic because he has gone from knowing nothing to believing nothing
– Maya Angelou in *The Truth in Words* by Neal Zero.

Optimism is the faith that leads to achievement; nothing can be done without hope
– Helen Keller, *Optimism.*

Don't be negative. It shows on your face
– Shahrukh Khan.

When the mind is conquered, the world is conquered
– Guru Nanak.

Air Element Chart

Main Animal	Birds	*Character*	**Nurturing, Fertile, grounding**
Direction	East (sunrise)	*Function*	Knowledge, Wisdom, Thought
Colours	Indigo, Violet	*Purpose*	Exploration
Metal	Silver	*Activities*	Breathing, journaling, organizing
Body	Breath	*Plant*	Eucalyptus
Season	Spring	*Astro Signs*	Gemini, Libra, Aquarius
Part of Body	Brain	*Angel*	Raphael
Function	Thought	*Archetype*	Old Person, Father
Mythic Beings	Sylphs, Pixies	*Power*	Projective
Part of Day	Dawn	*Musical Instrument*	Wind (Flute)
Temperature	Warm	*Places*	Plains, Skies, Towers, Airports, Schools, Libraries, Offices
Sense	Hearing, Smell	*Transition*	Student
Forceful	Hurricane, Tornado	*Season*	Spring (Sprouting)
Visible Form	None	*Body* Gland / System	Thyroid / Musularskeletal
State of Matter	Gases (oxygen, helium, air)	*Symbols*	Feather, apple, owl
Primary Symbol	Birds, Wings	*Geometric Symbol*	Hexagon
Deity	Athena, Hermes, Mercury, Zeus	*Affirmation*	'I think'
Gender	Masculine		

156

What Are the Characteristics of the Air Centre?

Location: You can picture the Air Centre as a circle from the forehead extending down to the throat. It encompasses the ears, the nose, and the voice box or larynx in the throat. The brain organizes thought, memory, concentration and imagination here.

Purpose: Here you overcome worry and plant the seed of belief in your thoughts, and in turn you develop your character qualities. Your character qualities here include wisdom, discipline and learning. Symbols are used to express these qualities. For the Law of Attraction your character determines what you attract into your life.

Air and Thought: Thought is associated with Air element because both are ethereal and light. Just as dark and soft clouds are formed by the winds, your thoughts can change from restrictive thoughts of limitation based on worry to liberated thoughts where you believe in yourself and the universe.

Visualization for the Air Centre:

1. Imagine the golden light from the Spirit travels down to the throat where it forms a circle of pulsating Indigo light.
2. This is the Air centre, which expands and encompasses the throat covering the face up to the eyebrows.
3. Imagine a hexagon shape within the circle, signifying combined energies of Spirit and Air.
4. Next affirm: 'I think' three times and each time imagine the Air centre pulsating with great energy as those words vibrate in your throat. Thinking is connected to 'I see, I speak,' as your thoughts arise from perception and give rise to communication. So consider the clarity of your perception and communication.
5. Linger for a few minutes at this centre and direct energy to activate its energy for your benefit.

Why Is Air Vital to The Law of Attraction?

Positive thinking and the Law of Attraction has largely operated at this centre because of the primary importance of thought in the transformation of your life. This is where you plant the Seed of Belief in your own mind. Other words related to belief are trust, faith, conviction and confidence

However, before you can plant, you want to remove weeds choking your mind with worry, doubt and negativity. The Law of Attraction states that 'like attracts like.' This means that your thought vibration, whether 'negative' or 'positive,' influences many aspects of your life. Your vibration is your *predominant character qualities* that you bring to all aspects of your life.

When you vibrate low character qualities, then over time your vibration can harm a relationship. However, when you act responsibly you will find, so long as your partner also takes responsibility, your relationship improves.

Similarly, in a job interview your character has a huge impact on how the interviewer perceives you. When you are comfortable with yourself, you naturally feel relaxed and confident. This enormously increases your odds of landing the job.

Take a moment now to think about an area in your life where you've experienced a challenge. What role did your character play? Are you taking responsibility for increasing your vibration?

Of course, some situations reveal less about you and more about those around you. For example, in a situation of abuse, neglect and wilful intention to harm by someone in your life, you are *not* responsible for their actions. Still your responsibility is to remove yourself from this toxic or dangerous environment.

This is not always easy but you want to trust your judgment and do what is best for you. You are responsible to take action to ensure your growth as a complete human being. Your friends, family, people and organizations in your community are often willing to support you during the transition. They also have a responsibility to help you whether they realize it or not. Know that whatever situation you are in, you always have hope. As Dr. Bernie Siegel reminds us, there is no such thing as 'false hope.' You need to affirm that you are deserving of the best in life.

The primary symbols for air are tied to flight, including birds, wings, feathers and fabled winged fairies, sylphs and pixies. Flight associated with Air represents the creative side of human thought and imagination, which allows you to rise above boundaries of Earthly realities and find full freedom to explore.

Importance of Raising Your Standard

Tony Robbins in *Awaken the Giant Within* shows the importance of raising your standards. Before you can do anything great or create the kind of life you dream of, you want to ask more of yourself. With this standard you can stay on course even when tempted to abandon your plan, dream or vision. Even when old attitudes and behaviours resurface, you can resist them because your focus is on growth. Try this exercise to reveal your standard:

Exercise to Raise Your Standard

Tony Robbins changed his life by raising his standard. He wrote down all the things he would no longer accept, and he also wrote down what he wanted to become in his life. You can also expect more from yourself and decide to live a fuller life based on your own measure of fulfillment. Here's how:

1. Take a few moments to become quiet and centered. Notice your breath and let it become nice and rhythmic without any effort, let yourself relax.
2. Once centered, write down the top ten things you want to change in your life. This can include health, relationships, direction, career, money and personal growth. Just write down what comes to mind until you have ten items.

3. If you can't come up with what you want, think about what it is you don't want. Then change what you don't want into what you do want. For instance, you don't want to be unable to pay your bills at the end of the month. Change this to: 'I want to be able to pay my bills on time each month.' Here are a few other examples:

I don't want to be alone	I want a satisfying relationship
I hate being sick	I want to be healthy
I don't like my job	I want meaningful work
I don't want to worry	I want to be confident

4. Now review your list and number it from one to ten. One being what you really, really want to change, and ten the least important item for you to change.
5. Consider your top three items on your list.
6. Now from these top three items, select one to focus on raising first. Once selected affirm to yourself: 'I dedicate all my thoughts, energies and efforts to achieve abundant flow of _____ [*state your top item here*].'
7. Send this thought vibration into the Universe and trust that the Universe will manifest your best.

What Are the Components of the Law of Attraction?

1. Believe and Develop Character

The Air centre is influenced by social conditioning, so carefully consider what *you* truly want. The dominant archetype for Air is *Explorer*. Through the powers of your thinking, you want to explore new ideas, horizons and possibilities. At first, your focus is brainstorming ideas without judgment. When you have come up with some options, then you can start to sift through them based on your own character qualities. What is the right direction personally for you?

Only you can ultimately decide what is right for you. Your character arises from your personal convictions, not from what matters to society or other people. This is an important distinction to keep in mind, especially at this stage where even helpful advice from others can discourage you from your confidence in an idea or even yourself. As writers we have found out that initially keeping an idea for a book hushed at first allowed for us to develop the idea on our own. If we opened the idea at this stage, even well-intentioned criticism of others may have kept us from pursuing our dream of writing.

With Air you want to **Believe** in yourself. Your primary task is develop self-confidence in who you are and in your inspirations. Your self-image determines your level of confidence in yourself. If you have a weak self-image, then you expect little from yourself and are willing to settle for minimum growth in your life. Growth of character in terms of who you are as a person is important, since you attract according to your character.

You vibrate your character qualities outwards and other people who resonate with your predominant character are drawn into your life. If you love, you attract loving people into your life. Conversely, a hateful person will attract like-minded people into their life. The sum of your predominant thoughts creates your character. So you want to focus special attention on your thoughts. You want to plant in your own mind the seed of strong thoughts, which lead to strong personal character qualities. These qualities are based on strong spiritual laws of development.

2. As You Sow, So You Reap

The kingdom of heaven is like a mustard seed that a man took and planted in his field. Although it is the smallest of all seeds, when it is fully grown it is the greatest of the herbs and becomes a tree, so that the birds in the heaven come and rest in its branches
– **Jesus**, Matthew 13:31–32.

As you plant, so you eat
– **Guru Nanak**, *Guru Granth Sahib*, 25-14

The Air centre is about taking personal responsibility for your thoughts in order to live to your full talents and capabilities. You reap character from your collective thoughts because over time thoughts become habits observed in behaviour. When you plant thoughts of integrity, courage, resilience, honesty, loyalty and patience, then you reap rewards in your character development.

Your character qualities determine what you attract in your life. For example, when you are sincere, honest and loyal in your interactions with others, then your relationships whether in business or personal life are enhanced.

3. Activate Your Intentions

Through visualization exercises, meditation, archetypes, symbols and the creation of a space or room, you *activate* powerful intentions across all Elemental Centres. As you make your intentions visible through images and objects that carry strong emotional connection for you, the Self is transformed. At the Air centre, images and objects associated with wisdom, exploration, discovery and communication are used to transform character.

4. Be Open to Receive

A limited way to understand openness to **Receive** from the Universe is to have your hand out to receive goodies that you want. However, your relationship with the Universe is two-sided where the Universe is blessed by your service and where you are blessed by the inspiration offered through Spirit.

You have a co-creative relationship with the Universe based on a real partnership. *At times the Universe may grant your wishes and on occasions the development of your character requires another path.* You are open to receive all and whatever you receive you are thankful, for every gift offers an opportunity to develop your character qualities.

When you receive what you want and you are blessed with wisdom, then you will use your gift for your benefit and the benefit of others. However, if you receive other than what you wished for, you need to consider how this is also a blessing. How is this a gift to help in your growth? Are you learning to exercise patience, persistence, or consider another direction?

Your character is developed when you consciously approach life with a view to self-growth. Even if all you want is money, you still need to develop character; otherwise all that you acquire will soon be squandered.

So here is our formula for the Law of Attraction in four phases:
+ Spirit
+ Believe
+ Activate
+ Receive

It's All in Your Attitude

Your overall character creates a predominant attitude to yourself, to other people, to life, and to the Universe. Dr. Bernie Siegel, the author of *Love, Medicine and Miracles*, has studied the attitudes of terminal cancer patients for many years. He noticed a trend with those who turn their life around and live for years. They chose to live their life in spite of their illness instead of feeling helpless. Why does attitude play a huge part in your life?

Well, over time repeated thoughts create your character, and your character forms attitudes in your mind. If you've made a habit of being grumpy each day, as this attitude compounds, it forms your predominant character. Your character determines your self-image and your level of confidence determines your response to life. If you have low self-confidence or an over-inflated ego, often a character flaw lies at its core. Here is the pattern:

Character → Your Self-image → Level of Self-confidence = Your Response

For low self-image this is based on fault-finding where you decide that somehow you just don't measure up. You're too thin or too fat, too tall or too short, and so on. Often in a culture driven by how you look this can lead to unrealistic body image.

An over-inflated ego can lead to the other extremes with excessive pride, arrogance and mental stubbornness. In either case your mental picture of you is distorted. Both lead to worry with low self-esteem worry based on personal insecurities, for an over-inflated ego worry over being outdone by someone else.

If you are easily affected by thoughts of discouragement and failure, or have an excessively aggressive and competitive nature, then you want to shift your thoughts to a balance between confidence and teamwork. You can shift your thoughts, attitudes and form a new character ethic that balances co-operation with self-confidence. Your character is neither passive nor aggressive, since it can flexibly move between being self-confident and allowing, according to the situation.

What to Do About Worry?

Worry is something that accompanies you throughout your day. Even when you eat, worry can rob you of the pleasure of food because you worry about the calories and weight-gain. If you let go of the worry, truly enjoyed the food then emotional eating is naturally stopped. You need to turn your worries about money, food, shelter, and about the future to a Higher Power. The Universe provides for all creatures, whether great or small, and so provisions for your well-being are also given.

Two Parables on Abandoning Worry by Jesus

In Matthew 6:25-29 Jesus gives reasons about why to avoid worry and to have trust through two parables.

25 Therefore I tell you, do not worry about your life, what you will eat or drink; or about your body, what you will wear. Is not life more important than food, and the body more important than clothes?

Jesus asks you to leave worry aside for basic provisions, including food, drink and clothing. He places greater value on life than on any of these necessities because when you have life these things can be added to it. Life is much more than the sum of any of your possessions.

26 Look at the birds of the air; they do not sow or reap or store away in barns, and yet your heavenly Father feeds them. Are you not much more valuable than they?

This verse shows that worry is unnecessary because you trust that the Divine will provide. Your need to hoard based on worry of lack is replaced with trust, just as birds are confident of sustenance even though they do not plant, harvest or store food on their own. This does not mean that you do not plan for the future or save some of your money for a rainy day. What it is discouraging is need to hoard money because of fear and lack of confidence. The parable is encouraging confidence in God, for as the birds are provided for, your need will also be satisfied. This level of trust is necessary for your journey forward into expanding your life and for growth.

28-29 And why do you worry about clothes? See how the lilies of the field grow. They do not labour or spin. Yet I tell you that not even Solomon in all his splendour was dressed like one of these.

Clothing is associated with status and people can judge you by what you wear. Yet, here you are reminded that even when you wear fine clothes, natural beauty as exhibited by the lilies of the field still surpasses the finest clothes. So worry less about what adorns your body and know that you have a natural beauty that surpasses anything you wear. Teachings on overcoming worry are found in many spiritual and religious traditions. Guru Nanak also counsels on it.

Guru Nanak on Worry:

Why, O mind, worry about effort, when the Dear Lord provides? Under hard stone animals live, their nourishment before them is placed.
– **Guru Granth Sahib** 10-9.

Worry often makes you strive unnecessarily but when trust in the Universe is established, then you feel a sense of peace that your needs will always be met. Even animals that live hidden under stone receive sustenance by natural systems.

Plant a Mental Seed

Weeding of thoughts that lead to weak character is an essential part of the Air centre. The development of positive thoughts, a prevalent attitude, and a strong character are essential for weeding. First you plant a seed of belief in your mind of the kind of person you want to be and then character sprouts from it.

Sometimes due to resistance you will need to plant many seeds of belief before one takes root in your mental soil and puts out a shoot. As that shoot grows stronger, it represents the growth of your character through challenges and opportunities. First you till the soil to soften the ground of your thoughts and the seed can find a receptive place in which to grow. You till the soil through focused meditation and visualization. Here is an exercise to get you started:

Seeding the Mind Exercise

1. Consciously take a few deep breaths – breathing in vital air and breathing out tension.
2. Gently close your eyes and envision a mysterious old man or woman, an archetypal image providing wisdom and guidance to you as the Explorer, throwing seeds on the ground.
3. Some of the seeds fall upon dry soil, rocky soil and others fall upon previously tilled soil where they can grow.
4. Consider these seeds growing under the tilled soil and beginning to put forth tender shoots.
5. You notice that weeds of doubt, pessimism and anxiety are crowding out the tender stalk.

6. As your thoughts focus on the stalk, it begins to strengthen, grow and the weeds withdraw as light casts away shadows without any resistance or effort.
7. When you surrender to encouraging thoughts, the weeds of negative thoughts automatically decrease and release their hold on your mind.
8. Affirm to yourself: 'I plant the seed of positive thoughts in my mind. As I do so, the weeds of doubt, pessimism and anxiety diminish more and more.'

The seeds of your thought over time develop your character. As you focus your mind, control your thoughts, and gain self-awareness, you will develop virtuous qualities that create growth and prosperity in your life. You can tend to your mind with focus developed through specific meditation techniques.

How to Activate the Air Centre

1. Develop Focus

Singleness of purpose is one of the chief essentials for success in life, no matter what may be one's aim.
– John D. Rockefeller.

Whatever we put our attention on will grow stronger in our life
Maharishi Mahesh Yogi.

Through tending your mind you can form character qualities of tranquility, confidence and truthfulness. But when your thoughts are agitated, then confusion, insecurity and falseness may rule your mind.

Only when your thoughts are calm can you connect to your hidden Self, which lies outside of the roles and masks you wear in daily life.

When you know who you are authentically as Self, then your direction is clear as you drop the masks, which arise from your

167

roles in life. They can include role of a parent, child, spouse, employee, and many others. The first step to connect to the real you and activate the Air centre through focused awareness.

Practice Focus through Calming Meditation

In the Audio CD, *The Way to a Meaningful Life*, the Dalai Lama teaches Calm Abiding Meditation. In this meditation you focus your mind on a single object. Here are instructions adapted from His Holiness:

- First consider what will be your focus. You can focus on an object such as candlelight, symbol, or image.
- Take your seat for meditation either on the floor with a cushion beneath you or in a chair
- Keep your back straight
- Gently close your eyes and focus on your object
- Let your breathing and thoughts slow down, down and down
- Now visualize or imagine your selected object
- When your mind wanders, gently return to your object
- Do not push yourself. Start with a three to five-minute meditation session and slowly build up from there.

1. *Air Centre Archetypes*:

As the centre of wisdom, the Air centre is permeated with archetypes related to Character Development, Spiritual Guidance, and Exploration.

The Father archetype represents the conscious forces that control Air. He stands for tradition, development of moral character and self-control. These are the character qualities which are developed at Air. The image of God in Abrahamic religions, Judaism, Christianity, Islam, and other faiths, is cast as a Father image.

The Father figure is traditionally seen as distant and stern; offering planning, objectivity and discernment to his son or daughter. You can relate this image to your relationship with a father figure in your life. How would he advise you in making choices or selecting a direction in life?

The Wise Old Man or Woman is found in many forms as a teacher or in some cases trickster in fairy tales, legends, novels, and in movies.

The Wiccan Crone is a common feminine image of wisdom and represents the third aspect of the goddess after Maiden and Mother.

The Wise Figure is a symbol for mature growth of wisdom.

Other Examples

Other examples commonly found in culture include:

- Gandalf is a wizard in *The Hobbit* who starts the quest of the Bilbo Baggins to reclaim Lonely Mountain and its treasure from the dragon Smaug. In *The Lord of the Rings*, he is the guide to the Fellowship of the Ring in their quest to destroy the Ring in the fires of Mount Doom
- Obi-Wan Kenobi from Star Wars, who is a Jedi knight who trains Luke Skywalker to use the Force
- Merlin (Myrddin in Welsh) is a mystic wizard from the King Arthur legend, who enables Arthur's ascension and acts as his high counsel
- Fairy Godmother in fairy tales, who has magical powers to assist as a mentor or mother to help the person undergoing a quest. In Perrault's *Cinderella*, she appears when Cinderella weeps that she cannot attend the Prince's ball. So her Fairy Godmother uses magic to help Cinderella attend the ball.

The Air centre is connected to youth vitality and ideals and wisdom is necessary for growth and maturity of ideas. Both the Father and Wise Old Person archetypes represent guides for your psychological and spiritual development.

The Explorer is the archetype of the Self at this stage where you discover new thoughts, ideas and are drawn to travel. You want to learn about the world, explore great discoveries in various fields, and have a desire to learn and gain knowledge.

Learning and self-confidence in your abilities and in the inspiration that you find outside of yourself is central to being an Explorer.

A Visualization: Flying to New Heights

Gently close your eyes. Imagine or visualize an eagle soaring high in the skies, while you are down below standing on the ground looking up. You have a thought of how you wish that you can also fly, explore and have complete freedom as the eagle.

As you think this, your spiritual guide magically appears before you and grants your wish by waving his or her hands through the air. With that movement, you experience a buoyancy in your body, you feel as light as a feather, and your mind is uplifted from heavy thoughts that previously weighted you down.

Now imagine that you are transformed into an eagle and are soaring in the sky. As you feel the air under your wings, you are filled with Self-Confidence. You are now free to soar, explore and reach new heights with your thoughts and imagination.

2. Air Symbols

Angel Raphael	The angel Raphael presiding over Air represents healing, especially of vision. In Book of Tobit, he heals Tobit of his blindness. In thought mental images function similarly to clarify your vision of life. In Islam, he is called Israfil and is responsible for blowing the horn, sending out a 'blast of truth' to signal the coming of the Judgment Day. Your thoughts likewise function to clarify between integrity and deceit.
Crane	Crane represents wisdom and omens. Picture of a crane standing on a rock and gazing at the sun represents power of vision. You can incorporate a crane as a symbol of the wisdom.
Elephant	The largest land animal, elephants symbolize power, wisdom and courage. Their association with wisdom comes from their keen intelligence.
Bird	High-flying birds symbolize the Spirit but they also reflect the flight of imaginative thinking. They mediate between Spirit and Earth as does Air and thought.
Owl	Owls are associated with wisdom. The Greek goddess of wisdom, Athena (Roman Minerva) was often depicted with an owl. As owls can see well in the night, they are ideal symbols for wisdom.
Book	A symbol for knowledge, learning and scholarship.
Feather/Wings	Represents Air, realm of birds; also signifies Spirit
Garden	A cultivated garden stands for conscious mind represented by the Air element.
Head/Brain	A symbol of reason, intelligence and logic.
King or Queen	The monarch is a symbol of awareness, good judgment and discipline. The crown is representative of their authority and dominion over earth. Some famous monarchs today are the British monarchy, the king of Thailand, the king of Saudi Arabia, and the Emperor of Japan.
Peacock	The Peacock shows two sides of mind: 1. Glory and beauty 2. Vanity. In Hinduism, the peacock is associated with Lakshmi, the goddess of wealth.

Star of David	In Hebrew it is called *Mogen David*, 'Shield of David,' since it appeared on the shields of King David. King Solomon according to legend possessed a magic ring called 'The Seal of Solomon,' by which he communicated with demons. The ring came down from heaven with the name of God and this six-sided star engraved on it. It represents union of heaven and earth with two interlocking triangles. The triangle pointing up stands for heavenly energies and the downward-pointing triangle earthly energies. The Air centre brings energies of heaven and earth into harmony as thought and imagination link the intangible Spirit with concrete Earth. Today it is symbolic of Jewish identity and Judaism.
Sri Yantra 	Mandalas of Tibetan Buddhism are called Yantras in Hinduism. The Sri Yantra is the 'Great Yantra.' It shares many features in common with the Star of David, where upward and downward triangles represent Spirit and Earth energies. In the middle is a *bindu*, central point, where energies are harmonized The Sri Yantra also relates to male and female energies from which the Universe manifested.
Transpiration	All transpiration of Car, Ship and Plane represent Air as each one journeys through air.
Symbols Representing Technology, Science and Communication	Display any item symbolic of technological ingenuity and scientific discovery, including: Atomic structure, DNA helix, planets, beakers, test tubes, microscope, telescope, and miniature models of buildings, and a globe.
Hexagon	The Hexagon, along with Octagon, is a shape between a Circle with no sides represents the Energy of Spirit and four-sided Square represents the Energy of Earth. So Air or thought is the intermediary between Earthly and Spiritual existence just as winged birds and fabled winged beings can go between the solid Earth and the vast Skies.

Other Air Symbols: King Arthur, Books, Caduceus, Sylphs, Seed, Sophia, Owl, Diamond, Stork, Pegasus, Chimes

Create a Space Devoted to Learning

Character development or development of thought requires learning and reflection. If your home is missing a library or study area, consider designating a room or area for this purpose.

You can create one following these guidelines:

1. Consider whether you need quiet or think better with some noise in the background. Depending on your answer you want your space either in a quiet or low noise area.
2. Look at what room or space is ideal for study and reflection. Now start to convert it with placing a desk, computer, chair and reading books.
3. Make sure your desk, chair and computer are positioned properly for your body and height. Adjust your position until you feel comfortable.
4. Stock the space with supplies of pens, pencils, paper, dictionaries, thesaurus, books and any other tools you need.
5. Go through the list of symbols and pick those that best represent learning, wisdom and character development. You can also select from the list of symbols, those symbols that have personal meaning for you.

In case space is a concern for you, you can consider combining your Learning Space with your Meditation Room, integrating both functions into one space while maintaining the ability to focus on either one at any given time.

Moving From Air to Fire

You can work with higher values to guide your life, such as truth, beauty or love.

Your character is perfected when you pursue a higher goal in life. With the chapter on Air you learned how to believe in yourself and how trust in the universe as essential to your character development.

Through the character that you vibrate, you attract all into your life. As you move into the Fire centre, your work is to further expand character through the heat of devotion.

Bibliography for Chapter 6

Allen, James   *As a Man Thinketh*
Atkinson, William   *Thought Vibration*
Bradler and Scheiner   *Feng Shui Symbols*
Cirlot, J.E.   A Dictionary of Symbols
Dalai Lama   *The Way to a Meaningful Life* (CD)
Dyer, Wayne   *The Power of Intention* (CD)
Hanh, Thich Nhat   *The Miracle of Mindfulness*
Keller, Helen   *Optimism*
Maltz, Maxwell   *Psycho-Cybernetics*
Regardie, Isreal   *The Art of True Healing*
Robbins, Tony   *Awaken the Giant Within*
Siegel, Dr. Bernie   *Love, Medicine and Miracles*
Vitale, Dr. Joe   *Zero Limits*

Chapter **7**

Fire: The Heart of Everything

People will forget what you said
People will forget what you did
But people will never forget how you made them feel
– **Maya Angelou**

The greater your capacity to love, the greater your capacity to feel the pain
– **Jennifer Aniston**, Oprah Magazine, 2004.

When the power of love overcomes the love of power the world will know peace
– **Jimi Hendrix**.

Heal the world, make it a better place,
For you and for me and the entire human race,
There are people dying, but if you care enough for the living,
Make a better place for you and for me.
– **Michael Jackson**, *Heal The World* from *Dangerous*, 1991.

And in the end, the love you take is equal to the love you make
– **The Beatles**, *The End* from *Abbey Road*, 1969.

Love is the ultimate and the highest goal to which man can aspire
– **Viktor Frankl**, *Man's Search for Meaning*.

THE FIRE CENTRE

Main Animal	Lion, Desert Reptiles	*Character*	Energetic, Devotional, Loving
Direction	South (Most light)	*Function*	Purifying, Growth
Colours	Red, Orange	*Purpose*	Self-Transcendence
Metal	Gold	*Activities*	Light candle, bake, kindle fire, exercise
Body	Vital heat	*Plants*	Thorny, spicy or desert-dwelling
Season	Summer (Growth)	*Astro Signs*	Aries, Leo, Sagittarius
Part of Body	Heart	*Angel*	Gabriel
Function	Emotional Growth	*Archetype*	Orphan, Lover, Altruist
Mythic Beings	Salamanders	*Power*	Projective
Part of Day	Noon	*Musical Instrument*	Stringed (Guitar)
Temperature	Hot	*Places*	Deserts, Volcanoes, Fireplaces, Ovens, Saunas, Gyms
Sense	Sight	*Transition*	Youth
Forceful	House Fire	*Body Gland System*	Thymus Circulatory
Visible Form	Flame, Light, Neon Signs	*Symbols*	Flame, candles, sun, roses, stars, lightning, cactus
State of Matter	Plasmas & Fire (Sun, Stars, Lightning, Candles)	*Geometric Symbol*	Upward Triangle
Primary Symbol	Lover	*Affirmation*	"I Love"
Deity	Fertility goddesses		
Gender	Feminine		

176

The Loving Centre of Fire

Fire, as an element is unique since it is composed of three transformational components: Light, heat and burning.

The heat of Fire makes it both useful when controlled and destructive when aroused.

Fire is created from burning of fuel with the presence of enough heat and oxygen to create a chemical reaction, such as when wood is ignited by a spark and fed by oxygen. Once fire has started, flames and heat are produced.

The discovery of fire in prehistoric times provided heat against cold, light during the night and it cooked food. As settlements arose with the spread of agriculture, the fireplace became an essential part of a homely atmosphere. In a furnace of fire clay, iron and other metals were shaped into household items, tools and weapons. Hence fire is associated with tools and weapons.

The capacity of Fire to burn, melt and warm influenced many Ancient civilizations to consider this element as an essential symbol for personal transformation.

The sun as the source of life, light and warmth was worshipped as a god and many solar creeds arose in the world. Worship also extended to stars and lightning.

As sun, stars and lightning all contain light and heat, they have direct correspondence to the Fire element. Winged creatures associated with transformation, dragonflies, butterflies and mythic winged snakes, were also consigned to Fire.

Loving emotions are considered warm in nature, so Fire is linked with higher emotions purified by heat of trials. A common image of this is wandering in the desert, facing temptations and heat and starkness of the desert purifying your soul. The emotions are transmuted from lower to higher as Fire ripens your character, offering warmth and light for growth of seed into a sapling.

Fire is also related to trials, tribulations and suffering, which are considered searing in nature.

The seat of higher human emotions is considered the heart, which is why during Valentine's the shape of the heart is used to express emotions of love and passionate longing.

Fire and Previous Centres

Spirit gave Life, Air carried and planted a seed in the soil of your mind. Now at the Fire Centre that seed grows receiving warmth and light.

The growth occurs in your own heart as your heart opens to love, devotion and compassion. You move from 'I Am' consciousness of Spirit, to 'I Think' understanding of Air, and now to 'I Love' purity of Fire.

While love is full of roses it also contains occasional thorns, which form part of the pain and suffering of life.

Acceptance of unavoidable suffering that you must undergo is important to your growth.

Fire burns away your selfishness, excessive pride and ego-based impulses, leaving behind a pure expression of love. This love includes love of Self, Others, and a Greater Good.

Your character formation started with shifting your thoughts from negative to positive beliefs. Now your character formation enters actual practice of daily actions, of how you treat yourself and all around you.

The Heat of Fire

As loving vibrations grow, you send these vibrations to yourself with self-love and self-acceptance. Next, the vibrations are sent out to all around you. As you send them out, your own nature transforms from lower emotions of separation to higher emotions of union. Ultimately, fire allows you to transcend your ego.

At the Fire centre you learn that the Self is not only within but that the Self is formed, revealed and grows with your relationships.

Your actions reveal your true character, as how you treat others and yourself is essential for your development. Here is an exercise to help you to activate your Fire Centre:

Activate the Fire Centre

1. Imagine the Indigo light from Air descends to the region of the heart where the light changes to red and forms a circle of pulsating red light.
2. The circle expands to cover the heart and the surrounding areas of the chest around the sternum.
3. Recognize that Fire is associated with the heart, since it is considered the centre of emotions, love and higher feelings.
4. Within the circle, imagine an upward-pointing triangle showing that Fire transforms lower passions into higher emotions.
5. Next affirm the words: '*I Love*' three times and imagine the purity of the Fire centre glowing brighter with warm light each time.
6. Linger for some time at the Fire centre and consider what it means to love and to be loved. How devotion and compassion are best expressed in your life?

The Quest

Your quest at the Heart centre turns from ego-based impulses to the quest for the common good. There are three archetypes along a progressive continuum that define this quest. They are:

- **The Orphan:** When you first start out on the quest you are like an orphaned child, who has been hurt, abused or rejected by others. This causes great hurt, pain and anger. Until you release these emotions, emotional blocks of being orphaned will continue to enter your future interactions. You can release emotions associated with abandonment by taking responsibility for your life now. In order to grow, the Orphan says: *'I forgive and take responsibility'*

- **The Lover:** Once you are past blaming or feeling guilty for what happened in the past, you are ready to Love. The lover archetype incorporates aspects of play, romance and passion. Your self-image is contained in this archetype and affects your physical appearance. If you are critical of how you look, you will often deemphasize this archetype in your life. However, if you like how you look, you will connect to your energies as a Lover.
  The phrase for the Lover: 'I passionately love you.'

- **The Altruist:** The altruist is an archetype of a person filled with generosity, compassion and selflessness. Altruists help others without any expectation of reward because they are moved by a sense of service and universal compassion. Many caregivers, healers, aid-workers and religious figures exhibit the qualities associated with this archetype.
  The Altruist says: 'I devote myself to a higher cause.'

As you move from Orphan, Lover and Altruist, you are developing the ability to love with an open heart. Fire removes the past hurts, fears and hardness of heart through warming and activating higher feelings of love, empathy and compassion.

180

How Do You Connect to the Light?

An aspect of Fire is as Divine Light in the sense of illumination, enlightenment and clarification. Kabbalah offers an account of how to unite with the Light hidden inside the world. In the beginning was only Light but with creation this Light contained itself within the Spirit centre in order for the world to take form.

Still sparks of Light remained hidden in all the other centres below Spirit. Through love and devotion, these sparks are recovered.

The sparks are then revealed as always existing inside you and in the whole of creation.

Through connection to Light, you raise your purpose in life to a spiritual plane. Once raised, all your actions work toward a loving purpose.

Levi Yitzhak of Berdichev, a Hasidic teacher, shows how all activities in life can be spiritually elevated:

When you desire to eat or drink, or to fulfill other worldly desires, and you focus your awareness on the love of God, then you elevate that physical desire to spiritual desire. Thereby you draw out the holy spark that dwells within. You bring forth holy sparks from the material world. There is no path greater than this. For wherever you go whatever you do – even mundane activities – you serve God.

Your love in daily life can raise your devotional energy by which raw emotions are elevated and purified. Your centre shifts from self to include all in the Sacred Circle. This creates a dynamic synergy between your personal agenda and empathy for others.

A person who can harness personal and collective energies to a common goal can rise as a leader in business, politics and other areas of life. This requires connecting yourself to a cause, platform or issue larger than you. Then you use your abilities in service of that cause.

How Do You Elevate Character?

Rabbi Yehuda Berg, the founder of the Kabbalah Centre, in *The Power of Kabbalah*, offers a clear perspective of developing character based on Kabbalah. His Theory of Reactivity shows that reactive behaviour is based on the human desire to receive. This includes greed, selfishness, ego, exploitation, and other reactive impulses.

Yet underneath these tendencies, you seek fulfillment. Therefore spiritual transformation involves rising above reactive consciousness where raw emotions control you.

You transform from a Reactive Being to a Responsible Being. This change requires that you start to pay more attention to the choices you make. In a reactive state, you respond as if on autopilot to outside forces but when you are responsible you check how you react in any situation. This is what gives you choice and freedom in life.

With this choice you become empowered to make changes in all aspects of your reality from the inside-out. You have the freedom to stop reactive tendencies, since you control your response. Outside forces are not a valid excuse for reactive behaviour on your part. When you respond from a higher place of development, your character is then expanded.

When you commute, line-up at the supermarket, or wait at an office, you can decide your reaction. If you get angry or lose your patience, then you feel frustrated, disempowered and disappointed. You have forgotten that you control your inner state and response under all circumstances.

In contrast, responsible behaviour recognizes the situation for what it is and still takes responsibility for maintaining a relaxed inner state. If you react then the external situation, wins.
When you cease to react then you connect to the Light, a place of illumination and self-control.

So here is the Formula for Transformation of a Challenge:

1. A challenging situation arises.
2. Know the barrier is your reaction not the situation.
3. Assume total responsibility for your reaction.
4. Time works on your side because the time gap between the situation and your reaction offers choice. So pause before you take action.
5. Then open yourself to the Light and act responsibly for yourself and for others.

When you know that you have control over your response, your sense of responsibility grows. Your character is elevated as you consider your best response.

1. Start with Self-Love

Above all do not forget your duty to love yourself
–Søren Kierkegaard.

You will never be able to love anyone else until you love yourself. Even With your Fat Thighs!
– Leo Buscaglia.

The Orphan is that part of you that feels abused, neglected or hurt. These emotions create 'holes' in your heart that are healed through self-love and self-acceptance. After you can forgive yourself and others and take responsibility for the present moment, you start to open up to love.

The anger, hurt or pain is released from your body and emotional healing can occur. Only after this release can love enter your heart. You find union and remove feelings of separation. Love is always a choice and so it requires you to grow.

2. Love Those Around You

What we're all striving for is authenticity, a spirit-to-spirit connection
– **Oprah Winfrey** (O Magazine)

One does not fall "in" or "out" of love. One grows in love
– **Leo Buscaglia** (LOVE)

Romantic ideals of love ask you to wait for that ideal Romeo or Juliette to enter your life. Yet, while you wait you can develop patience, courage, forgiveness, and other character qualities of a Lover.

Loving another person involves stepping out of focus on you only, and into the perspective of the other person. You know when you really love because then you start to step out of your own concerns and focus on the other person and yourself in a balanced way.

Devote Yourself to a Greater Purpose

Whosoever offers to Me with devotion a leaf, a flower, a fruit, or water - that offering of love, of the pure of heart, I accept.
– **Lord Krishna** (Bhagavad Gita 9:26)

In Hinduism devotion to Lord Krishna is expressed by the ideal of devotion and selfless service. This same philosophy permeates many spiritual traditions and is found in business ethics.

The idea is to pursue a greater good beyond your personal goals and agendas. You remain carefree about the rewards of your actions. Your concern is devotion to a higher ideal, including to a deity, partner, loved one, or to a cause.

Compassion

Just as a mother would protect her only child with her life even so let one cultivate a boundless love towards all beings
– **Buddha** (The Discourse on Loving-Kindness)

Perfect kindness acts without thinking of kindness
– **Lao Tsu**

I believe that at every level of society the key to a happier and more successful world is the growth of compassion
– **Dalai Lama**

Kind words can be short and easy to speak but their echoes are truly endless
– **Mother Teresa**

Compassion can seem as an abstract concept but actually it is intimately woven with all your relationships. From a compassionate perspective, you ask yourself: 'What have I done to make the world a better place?'

One single act of kindness can make a big difference in someone's life. Your willingness to offer a hug, a gentle touch, a smile, a kind word, a listening ear, or a sincere compliment can make all the difference.

Compassion also asks that you accept others without judgment.

Before you criticize another consider that everyone has his or her own journey in life. So if you can help, then do so. Yet refrain from harsh judgment of them.

Unity

It's one world, pal. We're all neighbours
– Frank Sinatra.

We realize that all life is valuable, and that we are united to all this life
– Albert Schweitzer, *The Spiritual Life*

Down to the last link, everything is linked with everything else; so divine essence is below as well as above, in heaven and on earth. There is nothing else
– Moses De Leon, *Book of Zohar*

At your Spirit centre a vision of Unity characterizes experience, a sacred sense that all is one. This unity creates the connection to all life.

Compassion arises from this feeling of unity between all life, which Albert Schweitzer called 'Reverence for Life.'

This sense of oneness has inspired the humanitarian and ecological movements. It is also the basis for understanding between different cultures.

While human cultures are diverse, the basic experiences of life unite us with one another and with all living beings.

African Concept of Ubuntu

A traveller through a country would stop at a village and he didn't have to ask for food or for water. Once he stops, the people give him food, entertain him. That is one aspect of Ubuntu but it will have various aspects
– **Nelson Mandela**.

The concept of unity and empathy is found in the African concept of Ubuntu, which is a classical African concept present throughout Southern Africa. It is the founding principle of South Africa since Apartheid. Ubuntu includes the idea of unity, empathy, selflessness, respect, humanity, and being part of a greater whole.

The 2004 film *In My Country* starring Samuel L. Jackson and Juliette Binoche illustrated the idea of Ubuntu. The Zulu proverb *umuntu ngumuntu ngabantu*, 'a person is a person through other persons' captures the essential idea behind Ubuntu of bringing people together.

Devotion to Service

All things are our relatives; what we do to everything, we do to ourselves. All is really One
– **Black Elk**.

Happiness comes out of contentment, and contentment always comes out of service
– **Harbhajan Singh Yogi**.

It is high time the ideal of success should be replaced with the ideal of service ... Only a life lived for others is a life worthwhile
– **Albert Einstein**.

In this life we cannot do great things. We can only do small things with great love
– **Mother Theresa**.

Altruism based on compassion at its highest leads to service. For some this may lead them to work in medicine as a doctor, nurse or therapist. Through service you transcend your own plan and agenda, and engage in a noble work or cause. You want to alleviate suffering and do something to make the world better.

With or without financial compensation, you are rewarded for your service as it makes you feel more empowered when you can make a difference.

As you engage in something bigger than you, your own challenges are put in perspective. Service of others allows you to appreciate what you do have.

You also recognize that you are in fact blessed; and your gratitude leads to sharing with others. You can share your time, love and character qualities with others, not just money.

When you serve others often your own strengths are revealed in the process. Your thinking shifts from narrow interest to broader understanding of the world. Service is even more important than religious duties, which explains this saying attributed to the Prophet Muhammad:

Sometimes I enter prayer and I intend to prolong it, but then I hear a child crying, and I shorten my prayer thinking of the distress of the child's mother
– **Prophet Muhammad** (Fiqh us-Sunnah, Vol. 2, Number 51-b)

This spirit of caring is essential to service. Your concern for prayer or other concerns becomes secondary when someone needs your help. You turn your attention to their need.

Service is about recognizing a need and many service organizations started this way.

Service also includes Customer Service essential to business success where customers are valued.

If a company fails to make the customer feel valued, then customer loyalty is lost. That customer may also tell others to go elsewhere. So service is also important for business.

US President Barack Obama shows the importance of devoting yourself to a higher purpose:

Focusing your life solely on making a buck shows a certain poverty of ambition. It asks too little of yourself. ... Because it's only when you hitch your wagon to something larger than yourself that you realize your true potential
– Barack Obama (Knox College Commencement Address 2005)

What are you hitching your wagon to in life? Are you serving a great purpose, which gives meaning to your life?

Decide now to devote yourself to something or someone bigger than you!

Symbols to Use With Fire Element

Candles: They represent illumination and light.

Crystals: Symbols for reflecting spiritual energy and light.

Lights: This can include lamps, candelabra and menorah. All lights point the way to illumination and enlightenment.

Buddha Statue: Image for enlightenment and compassion. Devotion can also be directed to other teachers: Jesus, Moses, Muhammad, Lao Tzu or Nanak.

Chalice: The chalice of the Christian worship is a transcendent form of the cup. It is related to the Grail and its spherical nature points toward openness to higher forces.

Rooster: The rooster is considered a sun symbol and represents activity and alertness. In Christianity, it also came to signify the Resurrection.

Cross/Crucifix: Both have obvious associations with the sacrifice of Jesus. So it represents suffering and also hope of salvation through the resurrection.

Desert Images: Images of the desert due to its heat are associated with Fire and the sun's illumination.

Fire: The Fire element is associated with sun, heat, and flame with ideas of growth. Fire like water is a symbol of transformation and regeneration. Purification is a key part of the journey through fire as it burns away impurities.

Gold: The metal gold represents solar light and higher intelligence in the way of spiritual illumination.

The Sun Chariot: Tales of gods and traveling across the sky or sun in a chariot are frequent. A hero in the chariot represents the body consumed in service of a higher principle. The animals drawing the chariot depict qualities needed for completing the quest. So, the horses of Arjuna in the Hindu epic, *Mahabharata*, are white, signifying the purity of the driver, Lord Krishna.

The Grail: The grail is an intricate and beautiful legendary symbol of the Quest and a source of illumination.

Hawk: A symbol of solar transformation.

Heart: At the centre of the human body is the heart and so the heart became the repository of human emotions. The heart is the seat of love, devotion and compassion.

The Hero: The hero or heroine takes on the Quest for rising from lower to higher character qualities.

Jewels/Gems: Spiritual truths gained through character.

The Lamb: Purity, innocence, sacrifice and Jesus.

Lily: Symbol of purity and of Virgin Mary.

Lion: The lion is one of the strongest sun symbols, representing courage and strength.

Lotus: Symbol for the opening of the heart to love.

Pegasus: A winged horse representing transformation through the heightening of spiritual forces.

Salamander: The elemental creature associated with Fire.

Phoenix: A mythic bird that burned its nest with the ray's of the sun when death drew near only to rise again from the ashes. A perfect symbol for transformation and rebirth.

Stars: Show less intense light and illumination than the sun

Upward Triangle: The upward triangle shows energies going to higher purposes. It is the symbol for Fire element.

Winged Snakes/Quetzalcoatl: Winged snakes and the Aztec god Quetzalcoatl represent the transmutation.

Sun: The sun represents active, masculine forces of bright illumination, strength and courage. It is the source of life.

Swan: The swan symbolizes the Self in Indian traditions.

Sword/Weapons: Symbols of purification.

Thunderbolt: The action of higher forces on lower.

Treasure: Shows that striving leads to moral progress.

Unicorn: Symbol of purity, innocence and magic.

Venus: The Goddess of Love and sexual attraction.

Volcano: Symbol of controlling destructive side of Fire.

Wheel: The wheel is a solar emblem. The Buddhist Dharma Wheel represents compassion, while the Wheel of Fortune shows ups and downs of life as cyclical.

Create Your Social Space

To more fully activate the element of Fire in your life consider your social space; where you gather with others. In most homes, this is the living room, family room and dining room. So check these spaces out with the following guidelines:

- First rearrange the furniture in each space if people have trouble freely interacting with each other
- Place family photos, images of angels, saints or spiritual teachers in this space
- You can add other symbols linked with Fire here
- Add awards, souvenirs and artwork
- Add a bowl of fresh fruits on the dining table
- Use candles and lamps to provide adequate lighting

Bibliography for Chapter 7

Berg, Yehuda	*The Power of Kabbalah*
Besserman, Perle	*The Shambhala Guide to Kabbalah and Jewish Mysticism*
Buscaglia, Leo	*Born For Love*
	LOVE
	Speaking of Love
Cirlot, J.E.	*A Dictionary of Symbols*
Fromm, Erich	*The Art of Loving*
De Leon, Moses	*Book of Zohar*
Regardie, Israel	*The Art of True Healing*
Schweitzer, Albert	*The Spiritual Life*
Whitehurst, Ellen	*Make This Your Lucky Day*

Words of Wisdom...

After reaching new levels of awareness we are continually drawn into circumstances within the physical world to apply our remembrances, integrate them and offer this new awareness to others, thus manifesting Heaven on Earth
– Michael Mirdad

If you turn it over to the Universe, you'll be surprised and dazzled by what is delivered to you. This is where magic and miracles happen... The Universe will start to rearrange itself to make it happen for you
– Dr. Joe Vitale

*You can start with nothing
And out of nothing and out of no way,
A way will be made.*
- Michael Bernard Beckwith

Chapter **8**

The Flowing Waters

Take the time to do nothing. It will open up a completely new world of insight for you
– Scott Shaw, (Zen O'clock: Time to Be)

The big secret in life is that there is no big secret. Whatever your goal, you can get there if you're willing to work
 – Oprah Winfrey (O Magazine)

Flow with whatever is happening and let your mind be free. Stay centered by accepting whatever you are doing. This is the ultimate
– Chuang Tzu.

All our dreams can come true - if we have the courage to pursue them
– Walt Disney.

Make at least one definite move daily toward your goal
– Bruce Lee.

What Are the Characteristics of Water?

General Characteristics

Water flows from high to low and as it collects at lowest points, it is considered closest to Earth. So it is the most natural and humble of all the elements. Water flows around an object and flowing with the current is less effort than going against it.

Water is also about flexibility as it adapts to any container. Due to its depths, water also represents the subconscious where aspects of parts of your personality are kept hidden from conscious awareness.

The Water centre is located just below the navel centre. It is all about focusing your energies through willpower. Here you are watering your plant, which started as life at Spirit, took seed at Air, and grew under the warm heat of Fire. Now you are watering it with willpower.

The Water centre near your navel is your 'engine-room' where you derive power for all your activities in life. Physical, sexual and creative energies are important expressions of this centre. Maturity and character development here is about focusing your energy instead of dispersing it.

Element

Water is the element for the Navel centre. Importantly, the focus of the fourth energy centre is translating spiritual concepts into actions that create free flowing energy. Willpower and patience are also important aspects of this centre, which are demonstrated by the qualities of water. Water reaches its destination but is patient in flowing around objects in its path.

THE EARTH CENTRE

Main Animal	Fish	*Character*	Flowing, yielding
Direction	West (sunset)	*Function*	Purification, intuition, rest
Colours	Blue, Black	*Purpose*	Cleansing, subconscious, quenching
Metal	Silver	*Activities*	Bathing, swimming, relaxing
Body	Blood	*Plants*	Aquatic: water lilies, seaweed
Season	Autumn	*Astro Signs*	Cancer, Scorpio, Pisces
Part of Body	Belly	*Angel*	Michael
Function	Desire, Will, Strength	*Archetype*	Warrior, Animal
Mythic Beings	Undines/Merfolk	*Power*	Receptive
Part of Day	Dusk	*Musical Instrument*	Bowed (Violin)
Temperature	Cool	*Places*	Ocean, river, lake, beach, pool, bathroom, bedroom, spa
Sense	Taste	*Transition*	Adult
Forceful	Drought, Flood	*Season*	Fall (Harvest)

Visible Form	Water (H2O)	*Body*
		   Gland
		   System
			
			 Pancreas
			 Reproduction, Digestive, Urinary

State of Matter	Liquids (water, milk, blood, oils, juices, sap)	*Symbols*	Shells, water feature, sea, moon, lotus, Rain, Rainbows
Primary Symbol	Mother Earth	*Geometric Symbol*	▽ Inverted Triangle
Deity	Lunar goddesses	*Affirmation*	'I will'
Gender	Feminine		

Moon

Fire is associated with the sun, and water is associated with the moon due to relationship of the moon's gravity on the tides. The mysterious lunar cycles are related to feminine cycles of menstruation, pregnancy and menopause. So the moon is considered feminine in nature.

How to Overcome Fear?

Our deepest fear is not that we are inadequate. Our deepest fear is that we are powerful beyond measure. It is our light, not our darkness that most frightens us
– **Marianne Williamson**, *A Return to Love.*

In order to effectively translate spiritual concepts into actions, and thereby create a more free flowing energy for your prosperity and abundance experience, it is of paramount importance to overcome your fears. Before you can move ahead in your prosperity experience you must consciously and willfully let go of fear. Here you can see how manifesting prosperity is built on letting go. The more you let go of your fears, the stronger your foundation for manifesting prosperity will be.

There are two main types of fear: The fear of failure and the fear of abundance.

Fear of failure takes three forms:
1. Fear: 'I have nothing.'
    Overcome this by: If you have nothing to lose, then why fear? Any action you take will benefit you.
2. Fear: 'I have only a little to lose.'
    Overcome by: If you have only a little to lose, then that small loss can easily be recovered and you can learn from the experience.

3. Fear: 'I have a lot to lose.'
    Overcome by: In this situation, listen to the fear without becoming immobilized by it. Use your fear to learn about the risks and opportunities. Wisely make your decision after considering the risk and the potential for growth.

You may experience even a fear of success at a conscious or subconscious level. It's strange but true. Unless your self-image grows and you can see yourself in the successful life that you dream of, you will subconsciously sabotage your efforts. Deep down you are limiting yourself and so your subconscious finds ways to keep you from progress.

To overcome your doubts, think of all your efforts to get here, and then carry on into experiencing the success that you have worked toward. As you do so, you will experience transformation and move from fear to courage in pursuing your dream.

You might hang onto the 'safety-line,' which is the something you fear losing. An example of safety-line is holding a job that you have outgrown but you are afraid to let go. Cutting this safety line means you have to go outside of your comfort zone. This expansion offers growth but you need to release your fears of the unknown, trusting your potential for growth.

So as you release your fear of moving outside of your comfort zone, your new prosperity and abundance will manifest. In many cases, the underlying reason for procrastination is based on fear. When you move past your fear, your procrastination naturally dissolves as your inner archetype of Warrior regains courage.

The Warrior Within

The Warrior archetype represents hidden forces inside you. Patience, stamina and bravery are some of the tools used by a warrior for development of the Self.

The path of the warrior is sensible as effort is balanced with flexibility, gentleness with firmness. A quiet stream is powerful yet gentle in movement, so like water you should travel with ease in life.

The warrior is tough and courageous with a decisiveness that frees energies toward achievement of a goal. Taking the example of water, the warrior overcomes obstacles by going around them, submerging them by greater force, or taking a new path.

As a warrior, your battle is internal with your own instinctual drives. So here the warrior battles another archetype, the Animal.

The Warrior Versus The Animal

The symbolism of an animal can vary with the specific animal, correspondences and context. For example, a tamed animal is considered differently than the same animal in the wild. A domesticated cat is different than one in the wild.

Often the warrior or knight will encounter a wild or fabled animal like a dragon. The knight wins either by slaying or taming the animal. The death of the animal is symbolic of the moralistic triumph of human reason over animal instinct. The legend of St. George and the Dragon captures this idea.

St. George travelled for many months by land and by sea until he came to the town of Salone in Libya. Here he met a hermit who told of the distress of the people being terrified by a dragon. He added: 'Every day this dragon demands the sacrifice of a beautiful girl. Tomorrow Sabra, the king's daughter, will sacrifice herself, unless a brave knight can slay the dragon.'

St. George set out the next morning, to save the princess Sabra who was headed to sacrifice herself to the dragon dressed in the finest Arabian silk. He asked her to return to the palace. After she left, he entered the valley of the dragon.

The dragon roared from its lair louder than thunder but St. George was not frightened. A terrible fight ensued in which the dragon repeatedly tried to poison St. George. The dragon's attempts failed as St. George was protected by an enchanted orange tree. After resting under the tree and regaining his strength, St. George pierced the dragon with his spear and so he rid the countryside of the dragon's terrors.

This legend shows the importance of courage in taking on a calling. The challenge is a test of your qualities and your success strengthens your character. You are determined in carrying out your mission with your willpower but you are also open to accept help from a higher source.

The willpower is often misunderstood as arising from ego but the ego and the will are different. The ego is narrow, contracted and turned inward; in contrast, the will is open and expansive.

In the legend of St. George, the hero has utmost courage, yet during the battle he is open to receive protection from the enchanted tree. In the same way, in your struggles in your life, you need to face them courageously, yet be open to work with others.

In most of these tales of a warrior fighting an animal the victory is symbolic of virtuous life winning over lower instincts. The depth of instincts is symbolized by characteristics associated with the beast, including the elevation at which it resides. So high-flying birds and other winged creatures are associated with higher spiritual energies but creatures further below are considered instinctual in nature.

Animals that shed their skin like the snake or undergo a metamorphosis like the butterfly represent the transformation of lower into higher nature. The *butterfly* has been an emblem of the Self. The evolution from a lowly, flightless caterpillar to a beautiful winged butterfly heightens its symbolic value for transformation and growth. Fabled creatures that are half human, half animal vividly depict the struggle between instinctual and moral life.

Human/Animal Halves

With fabled creatures the instinctual nature is indicated by what constituted animal and human in their bodies. So with *centaurs* the lower half is animal composed of horse and the upper half is human. So centaurs had reasoning capacity like humans but below they were influenced by instinctual drives.

This is why in myths, they are warlike and troublesome, except for Chiron, who contrary to his kind was intelligent, cultured and compassionate. The rational capacity is present in centaurs but because of uncontrolled base desires and urges, most are unable to morally transcend their violent and disruptive nature. The centaur is used in astrology as the symbol for Sagittarius.

With the *minotaur* the instinctual desires dominate the creature, as the lower half is human but the upper half is a bull. While the centaur is monstrous in its lower half, it still has reasoning capacity.

The minotaur, however, is a complete reversal as instinctual urges have overtaken the head, including mental functions of reason, creativity and imagination.

Rescued by Animals

The struggle with an animal is not always adversarial in stories. Many stories tell of people being rescued by animals such as dolphins.

According to legend, the Greek poet Arion was miraculously rescued by dolphins after being kidnapped by pirates. Arion was kidnapped by pirates who wanted to steal his rich prizes that he had won from a musical competition in Sicily.

Under threat of death, Arion asked for a last wish to sing a song, which the crew granted. His song fascinated dolphins, who rescued him from drowning as he threw himself into the sea. He was returned safely to shore by the friendly creatures.

In these stories, the animal and human figures have a relationship based on higher emotion of friendship, compassion and helping. The animals here symbolize the control of instinctual nature through higher emotions directing actions.

Even in stories adversarial in nature, often the animal is tamed instead of being killed, which points to the importance of controlling and directing your desires, not being overrun by them.

Drowning in the Waters of Desires

Water has twofold nature: One of purification and the other of drowning. When water is controlled or directed, it can be used to cleanse and religious ceremonies use water for such purposes in baptismal ceremonies, washing before prayers in Islam, and in pilgrimages to sacred rivers such as the Ganges in India.

Rough waters represent undirected desires, which lead to a life without meaning, purpose and direction. In order to focus your energies, a clear intention is needed based on the exercise of your willpower. Otherwise, the image of drowning in waters depicts the state of someone whose desires have controlled them. You need to master your desires, instincts and urges, and direct them to a goal in life. While you can crave many things, you need to explore what is really worth pursuing in your life and what is merely passing gratification. By doing so, your character matures from infantile need for constant stimulation to knowing that your life has a greater purpose. The idea of getting caught in desires is also depicted in getting entangled in the net spread over the world-ocean in India.

Exercise to Clarify Your Purpose

If you find that you need a clear focus for what you really want in your life, this exercise is designed to help you:

1. Breathe deeply into your belly for a few breaths, allowing yourself to relax.
2. Imagine or visualize a bright blue circle over your entire abdomen, pulsating with power.
3. Now in the middle of this circle is an inverted triangle pointing down, showing the energies from your sexual organs and drives. These potent sexual energies are raw.
4. You decide to harness the sexual energies and direct them upward toward the Water energy centre just below your navel. The energies are of a dark hue and when they flow

upward to the Water centre they commingle with the lighter glowing blue there.

5. As the sexual energies collect at the Water centre, you can experience your willpower increasing at the navel centre and you feel charged.
6. You ask your will: 'What are my intentions? What do I truly want in life?'
7. Let the answer come to you from the depth of your subconscious, visualized as located in your gut.
8. Consider where you will direct your energies in your life.
9. Now focus all your energies to achieve this transformation and utter the words 'I will' three times. Each time the Water centre pulsates with energy.
10. Take a deep breath and relax, allowing any tension to dissipate. With your intention clarified, allow the Universe and others to help you in your pursuit.

From a psychological perspective, the animal nature is your own instinctual nature based on appetites and desires. So when you clarify your intentions, you can embrace your desires while also directing them to higher purposes. As you do so, the animal symbolism previously based on a dichotomy of higher and lower can yield to friendship and act as a spiritual guide.

Your Animal Guide

The animal symbolism is closely associated with shamanism, animal worship and totemism. A totem is an animal that represented and protected a group of people in a tribe or clan. These animal spirits became important as spiritual guides with qualities that helped in self-development. For instance, the strength of a bear through symbolic association with that spirit guide can become part of your own character.

For anyone interested in their own animal guide, consider these questions:

1. Are you drawn to a particular animal? This can be any animal: Bird, fish, insect, reptile or mammal.
2. Does a particular animal seem to appear in your life?
3. Are you drawn to or frightened by certain animals?
4. Does a certain animal often appear in your dreams?
5. Are you fascinated by a visual image of a certain animal?

Also consider if you are drawn to these common animal guides:

Animal	Characteristic	Animal	Characteristic
Ant	Self-discipline	Fish	Sacrifice
Bear	Strength	Butterfly	Transformation
Beaver	Intuition	Frog	Rebirth
Bee	Industrious	Horse	Stamina
Cat	Mystery	Seahorse	Patience
Crab	Rebirth	Seal	Playfulness
Deer	Purity	Otter	Mischievous
Dog	Loyalty	Snake	Cycle, healing
Dolphin	Intelligence	Turtle	Endurance
Crow	Mystery	Whale	Wisdom

Common Symbols Associated with Water

Symbol	Characteristic	Symbol	Characteristic
Animal	Instinct	Lama	Cruelty
Apple	Temptation	Lake	Subconscious
Bathing	Purification	Night	Potential
Belly	Intuition	Ocean	Universal life
Boar	Indulgence	Ogre	Cruelty
Bridge	Transition	Rain	Purification
Clouds	Fruitfulness	Rainbow	Optimism
Crocodile	Power	River	Passing time
Crow	Messenger	Spider	Malice
Cyclops	Instinct	Sea Monsters	Challenges
Deluge, Flood	Purification	Sri Yantra	Union
Dew	Illumination	Yin-Yang	Union
Griffin	Protection		

Rooms Associated with Water:

Bedroom

The Bedroom has a two-fold purpose as the place of rest and passion. So when looking to add more flow into either aspects, you want to carefully examine the space in terms of both roles.

This chapter has discussed controlling desires but this is different from elimination of desires. Rather this is about focusing your desires, knowing what is most important to you and directing your energies there.

If you want more passion in your love life, then you direct more energy to your relationship for this purpose by placing items in your bedroom with intention. Here's how:

How to Add Passion and Rest to Your Bedroom:

If you have found someone special in your life or are looking to find your mate, then here are some suggestions:

1. Remove clutter from the bedroom and consider what theme, colours and items appeal to you and will harmonize the space.
2. Have the bed not in-line with the door, and have it accessible
 from both sides with two bedside tables on either side. Make sure the bed is comfortable with warm colours, pillows and soft sheets. You need to create space if you are looking to invite someone into your life.

3. To keep energy flowing, keep the area under the bed uncluttered.
4. Eliminate TV, computer or exercise equipment from the bedroom, since your focus is on love. Or add a divider or partition between the bed and that equipment.
5. Make sure the air and temperature in the bedroom is ideal.
6. Have a way to control the lightning level with a dimmer switch or a lamp that can be controlled.
7. Use soothing flesh-tone colours with accents from the red spectrum.
8. Add paintings and images that depict romance and love. For example, this can be a pair of two animals, deities or figures such as two swans, dolphins, Shiva-Shakti, etc. You can also consider adding a symbol expressive of union, such as the Yin-Yang or Sri Yantra symbols. When you add this object, you express an intention to attract or enhance love.
9. Remove any picture that depicts loneliness, sadness or isolation. If you have photos or letters from a previous relationship, consider letting them go. Before you bring someone new into your life, you need to emotionally and psychologically release the old bonds.
10. Add candles that are made from soy, palm or beeswax with cotton wicks to avoid smoke.
11. Use oil burner, potpourri, sachets, incense or fragrance to add warm, soothing and sensual aromatics to the air. Experiment with rose, sandalwood, vanilla, ylang-ylang and other scents to find one right for you and your partner.
12. Add ambient, sensual music that both of you love.
13. Also love yourself and take care of your mind and body with exercise, proper nutrition and meditation.
14. For rest it is highly important to remove any electric equipment from the bedroom due to vibrations emitted by it.

Bathroom

The bedroom and bathroom both play a role in rejuvenation and rest. So when you want to find ways to relax more in your life, consider both rooms and activities together. Water is perfect for relaxing the mind, body and soul.

So work with the bedroom to create your ideal place of rest:

1. Add a visual piece that delights or relaxes you.
2. Have enough mirrors for you to see yourself.
3. Make sure the room is well-lit from above and the sides. Add candles for when you want to relax with soft light.
4. Have colours that are relaxing and speak of purity. White, blues and soft colours are ideal here.
5. Select the right scents depending on whether you want romance, rejuvenation or healing.
6. Place crystals in the bathroom or any room to charge the energy there. Fix any plumbing problems to avoid shifting the relaxing vibes into frustration.
7. In China, flowing water is associated with wealth, so keeping the drains closed is considered a way to keep energy and money from going down the drain.
8. Keep the bathroom door closed and the toilet lid down when not in use to keep the energy in your home.

Cleansing Waterfall Visualization

Imagine that you are on a beautiful tropical island with no one around you. You hear a beautiful waterfall rushing down from a cliff into a lagoon. This is a healing sanctuary among the trees on a beautiful sunny day and you hear the birds joyfully chirping.

You decide to remove your clothes and swim to a rocky platform under the waterfall. Once standing under the waterfall, the gently rushing water envelops you with a delightful energy and vitality.

As you relax under the waters, you notice all the tensions, fears and anger leaving your body with the flow of the water.

The water also cleanses you and strengthens you, removing all toxic elements from your body. Spend as much time under the waterfall as you want. Afterwards, you feel relaxed, cleansed and invigorated, carrying those feelings into your day.

From Water to Earth

You have moved from all the centres above to Water where you have learned the importance of willpower, self-control and clarifying what you really want.

Now, as you move to Earth, your practice will come to full fruition, as the plant that began life from Spirit will bear fruit.

Those fruits will flourish based on the character you have developed with Spirit, Belief at Air, and Activation of your character at Fire and Water.

At Earth, you can experience the abundance of the Harvest.

Bibliography for Chapter 8

Cirlot, J.E.   *A Dictionary of Symbols*
Bradler and Schneider   *Feng Shui Symbols*
Radaj, DeAnna   *Designing the Life of Your Dreams from the Outside In*
Shaw, Scott   *Zen O'clock*
Whitehurst, Ellen   *Make This Your Lucky Day*
Williamson, Marianne   *A Return to Love*

Chapter 9

The Abundant Earth

My soul can find no staircase to heaven unless it be through earth's loveliness
- **Michelangelo**.

When we heal the earth, we heal ourselves
– **David Orr**.

The greatest glory in living lies not in never falling, but in rising every time we fall
– **Nelson Mandela**.

Today, we are truly a global family. What happens in one part of the world may affect us all
– **Dalai Lama**, 1989 Nobel Lecture.

If you tell me that you desire a fig, I answer you that there must be time. Let it first blossom, then bear fruit, then ripen
– **Epictetus**, *Discourses*.

Characteristics of the Element Earth

Upon earth you live and from Mother Earth you derive your sustenance just as a baby is fed and nurtured by the mother in the womb. So too your existence arises from the earth, which sustains and grounds you. Earth gives practical purpose to all previous energy centres:

- Infinite 'I Am' Consciousness of Spirit is *restricted*
- Optimistic 'I Think' Belief of Air is *grounded*
- Warm 'I Love' Emotion of Fire is *matured*
- Strength of 'I Will' Desire of Water is *contained*

THE EARTH CENTRE

Main Animal	Terrestrials	Character	Nurturing, Fertile, grounding
Direction	North (darkest)	*Function*	Burying, Planting
Colours	Green, Brown	*Purpose*	Fruition
Metal	Gold	*Activities*	Sculpting, gardening, hiking, golfing, cooking
Body	Flesh, Bones	*Plants*	Patchouli, Moss, Lichen, etc.
Season	Winter	*Astro Signs*	Taurus, Virgo, Capricorn
Part of Body	Feet	*Angel*	Uriel & Haniel
Function	Physical Body	*Archetype*	Gaia, Mother Earth
Mythic Beings	Gnomes, Dwarves	*Power*	Receptive
Part of Day	Night	*Musical Instrument*	Percussive (Drum)
Temperature	Cold	*Places*	Forests, Gardens, Fields, Caves, Valleys
Sense	Touch	*Transition*	Mature
Forceful	Earthquake	*Season*	Winter (Dormancy)
Visible Form	Matter	*Body*	
		Gland	Adrenal
		System	Musularskeletal
State of Matter	Solids with clear shape and volume	*Symbols*	Salt, Rocks, Clay, Wheat, Acorns, Square, Gardens, Wood, Soil, Plants, Food
Primary Symbol	Mother Earth	*Square Symbol Pictured*	
Deity	Fertility goddesses	*Utterance*	'I Bless'
Gender	Feminine		

212

Earth is where all the energies from Spirit, Air, Fire and Water previously activated are now released. The energies from all centres are collected, and finally bear fruit. At times they bear fruit quickly; at other times this is a process where the energies are refined through your character development.

The Universal Mother Archetype

While money and material growth are important with Earth, the objective is for enhancement of all areas of your life. As your money grows, you invest it in yourself and others, not to simply respond out of fear or greed.

The Mother archetype as expressed in Mother Earth or Mother Nature depicts the nurturing qualities associated with Earth energies. This means that you want to nurture growth in your life, yet your aim is focused upon well-being of all, not limited to personal interests.

The archetype of the Mother is inclusive in nature, embracing a concern for the welfare of Self, Others and for the planet Earth.

So with a broad worldly focus, the Earth centre connects you to wealth, health, ecology, environment, finances and social upliftment. Money is only one part of wealth, since *well-being* also includes money, prosperity and happiness.

As money is important to create growth on Earth, your responsibility is to develop character qualities that can enhance the process of creating abundance in your life.

Total Wealth

When people measure wealth, they often look at money and investments. But this is misleading as it says little about total wealth.

Total wealth includes many other aspects of life besides money. It includes wealth or well-being of all these components featured in the chart on the next page:

Component	Element	Location	Affirmation	Rooms/Spaces
Spiritual	Spirit	Crown	'I Am'	Meditation
Psychological	Air	Brain	'I Think'	Study, Library
Relational	Fire	Heart	'I Love'	Family, Living & Dining Rooms
Intuitional	Water	Belly	'I Will'	Bedroom, Bathroom
Physical	Earth	Feet	'I Bless'	Garden, Rec Room, Kitchen

When any aspect of well-being is missing or decreased in your life, then life as a whole can feel empty even with a lot of money or possessions. So consider how you will enrich each of these aspects in your life:

Element	Archetype	Description	Envision
Spirit	Child / Self	Joy, Bliss, Sacred	Heavens, Circle
Air	Father, Old Person, Explorer	Thinking, Imagination, Exploration	Sky, Feather, Birds, Light
Fire	Lover / Altruist	Love, Devotion, Purification, Compassion	Sun, Stars, Heart
Water	Warrior / Animal	Will, Intuition, Passions, Cleansing	Moon, Ocean, Animals
Earth	Mother / Gaia	Body, Material, Nurturing, Grounding	Earth, Plants, Man, Woman

Each centre offers wealth in the development of Self as follows:

Spirit

Spirit as Infinite, Complete and Whole offers you *Self-worth* and validates your existence as a Child of the Universe. This worth is something with which you were born, it is still with you, and it will always remain constant.

You can never lose it, no one can steal it, it cannot be burned in fire, drowned in water, or be buried under the earth. Yet in your thoughts you can forget your own worth and create a false image of yourself.

Air

At the Air center, you create a Self-image of who you are based on beliefs about yourself that often are expressed in your inner self-talk. When you change what you Believe, then your Self-image also shifts. Ideally, your thought would reflect the purity of Self as a clean mirror.

Yet, with specks of negative thoughts the reflection is distorted, which results in a false Self-image where you start to believe in yourself as limited. Your journey with Air is to use your thinking and imagination to rise above your limits as a bird can soar high in the skies.

You want to create *Self-confidence* at the Air centre through transformation of what you believe at the vibrational level of thought.

Fire

With the Fire centre, Self expands as love and devotion to a cause, person or living beings and leads to *Self-transcendence*.
The Self expands through social interaction and you find purpose to life outside of yourself in something or someone greater than you alone. Sometimes transcendence requires purification

through Fire, going through the dark night of the soul, where pain, loneliness and suffering are deeply experienced.

Yet, as a Hero learns to journey through life with devotion to a greater cause, you can also rise above your pain through healing.

Or you inspire others through the dignity and courage with which you suffer. Many individuals with disabilities have shown great courage in facing and overcoming their challenges. Their life becomes an inspiration for anyone else looking to live a full life. At Fire you are a Lover, who cares for all your relationships as a partner, parent, friend, and through spiritual devotion.

As this love expands to a universal level, the Lover turns into the Altruist, whose transcends the Self through service to all beings.

Water

At the Water centre, the shadowy depths of the subconscious are mined, allowing for an integration of intuitive hunches with conscious thoughts. What was previously hidden is allowed to rise to the surface, including your appetites, urges and sexual drives, represented by the archetype of the Animal.

When these raw animal instincts are of an entirely destructive nature as in the case of mythical poison-breathing dragons, then the Warrior in order to cleanse the Self kills the animal within, allowing for peace to emerge. In most cases, animal instincts are beneficial. So they are channelled as guides to intuitive awareness.

This leads to *Self-acceptance* of disowned parts of your psyche and to a more powerful integration of your energies. The expression/activation of these energies is essential for the Law of Attraction to manifest, or else your work will only be at a surface level with little exploration of deeper layers of the Self.

Earth

Lastly, at the Earth centre, you gain *Self-awareness* through an integration of your work at all the other centres.

At the Earth centre, you balance the development of the Self with practical, grounded awareness of manifesting all your needs on planet Earth, including participation in social, political and financial spheres.

The bodily image of man or woman represents the natural forces of Earth and the pentagram, along with the integration of all the elements as shown in the above illustration by Agrippa.

Through the Mother archetype, you nurture your own growth, the growth of other creatures, while respecting the ecological and environmental balance of the planet Earth represented as Gaia. So here is the journey of Self through all the Elemental Centres:

Spirit	Self-Worth
Air	Self-Confidence
Fire	Self-Transcendence
Water	Self-Acceptance
Earth	Self-Awareness

The practical nature of Earth also tends to your financial growth through Self-awareness of your values and needs. As you grow and your needs change, accordingly you change your financial portfolio. As you activate the Earth centre you come into full maturity, as you combine your inner work with outer transformation. You are excited by the prospect of taking your inner gifts and bringing them into fullest expression in the world. A way to express your gifts is through your achievements in life.

How to Express Your Gifts

Ideally what you pursue in life as a hobby, service, occupation or business venture is an expression of your gifts. When you pursue an endeavour fitting to your character, you are fully engaged in your pursuit – if it's anything less, you might feel constricted.

Robert T. Kiyosaki in *Rich Dad's Cashflow Quadrant* mentions four sources of income. The left side is centered on self-effort; while on the right growth of money is through management of people or money. Here are the four possibilities:

Left-side		*Right-side*	
Employee	Earn pay-check based on working for an employer	**Business Owner**	Owns a system by which business can grow
Self-employed	Pay depends on self-effort	**Investor**	Makes money by investing money

Each of these quadrants can meet your financial needs for the present and with discipline in spending within a budget, and saving and investing the rest of your money even as an employee you can create steady wealth.

However, your wealth is taxed right from your pay and in many cases your income just barely covers your expenses, or to afford larger purchases you need to place yourself in debt through student loans, car loans, mortgage and credit card debt. So you can do satisfactorily as an employee so long as you earn enough to live, cover your expenses, and have at least a bit extra for savings and investment. Still, discipline is highly important if you are to do well long-term as an employee because you need to take responsibility for nurturing and growing your money over time.

For those who rely on their own effort as a skilled tradesperson, specialist or consultant, self-employment can be rewarding. It offers independence where compensation is equal to your efforts.

The downside is that self-employment can take up a lot of your time because any growth in business means you have to work harder to keep up with the demand. To avoid this whenever possible you want to structure your business according to clear systems and procedures that anyone can follow. That way when you have a thriving business, you can hire employees instead of having to take more work on yourself. This makes the transition from a small-business to a big-business owner so much easier.

If you have money or access to money along with solid knowledge and experience in running a business then you can look into starting a big business.

To be a successful owner of a big business, you need the ability to look at the large picture. For example, you need the ability to read numbers and know how they affect your business decisions and planning for the future. You need knowledge, trustworthiness with money, and self-confidence in order to successfully create and build a big business. Character plays an important role here because people will invest in your business only if they have confidence in you.

The final quadrant is that of an Investor where you look to invest your money in stocks, bonds, real estate, your own business, or other financial vehicles. Where you invest your money depends on what investment makes most sense to you. You can invest in education, real estate, retirement savings plan, stocks, bonds, mutual funds, GICs and other investments. Depending on your values, knowledge and the type of investor you are will determine what is included in your investment portfolio.

The traditional approach of diversification in investments makes sense as general principle for investing. It is mentioned in the Talmud (Bava Metzia 42a), which recommends dividing your investments into one-thirds between business, cash and real estate. However, *diversification* is only one well-known strategy, another approach is value investing.

One of the most successful investors, Warren Buffet, CEO of Berkshire Hathaway, believes in *value investing* where you look to invest for long-term sustainable growth. His style of investing is narrowly focused on a few top companies instead of diversifying; he concentrates his investments on companies that offer long-term value. His advice is that if you have solid financial understanding, then concentrate your investments but if you have general knowledge then diversification makes sense.

You invest in those areas where you are good and which agree with your values. For example, if you're most comfortable with real estate and it makes sense to you then you concentrate your investment there, including spending time learning about properties and real estate market in your area.

The four quadrants offer many possibilities for increasing your means by creating income from a number of sources. That way your income will not be limited to just being an employee. Your investments or business will also make money for you.

Before if your income is limited then before you can invest in your own business or in investments, you need to discipline yourself in your spending habits in order to create savings and then to have money for future investments. First you need to create a budget, which is essential to awareness of your financial picture.

How to Create Your Own Budget

1. Collect bank statements, investment accounts, bills and pay statements together and write down total monthly net income
2. Record a list of your monthly fixed expenses like mortgage or rent, car payments, cable/internet, credit card payments
3. Write your variable expenses which change each month such as groceries, gas, dining out, entertainment and shopping
4. Total your monthly income and expenses
5. Adjust your expenses to balance with your income
6. Every month review your budget and update it

How to Nurture Savings

At the Water centre, your character development focused on having the willpower of a Warrior, which allows you to slay certain urges and focus your energies toward growth. Those same principles apply to discipline of your spending habits. Here is an exercise for Self-awareness of your monthly expenditures:

1. Check your monthly spending on your bank statements
2. Categorize your spending under three headings:

Essential Needs	What I Value	Optional Spending
Rent/Mortgage	*Whatever you value*	*Any discretionary*
Utilities	*goes here whether*	*or reckless*
Food	*it's kids, education,*	*spending.*
Transportation	*health, etc.*	

3. Check if you can cut $50-$200 in Optional Spending column.
4. You can also eliminate or reduce costs of:
   a. Costly and unhealthy habits: Smoking, gambling or drugs.
   b. Excessive drinking and reduce/eliminate meat, which is bad for the environment and costs more than a vegetarian diet.
   c. Spending money on brand names where you pay for advertising costs not better value.
   d. Minimize dining out or have water instead of drinks.

5. Automatically deposit the money saved in a savings account.
6. Build three to six months worth of savings
7. Open an investment account and automatically deposit into it.
8. When investing, select a lending investment: Bond, GIC, Stock, or an Ownership Investment: Business or Real Estate.

Saving in this way can take time, so your character is revealed in disciplining yourself with your spending, automatically putting the extra money into savings, and keeping your hands off that money and letting it build. Once you do so, take pride in your achievement of taking responsibility for your finances. Now you are putting money in your savings for a rainy day.

Once you have enough money in savings accounts, ideally three to six months worth of your living expenses then you can start to invest your money. For large purchases such as family vacation, large household items, car, or house you can create a savings account for that purpose, so that instead of going into debt you can use cash to purchase it or make at least a large downpayment.

What Is Good Debt And Bad Debt?

Just as the rich rule the poor, so the borrower is servant to the lender
– Proverbs 22:7

As part of your ability to nurture financial wealth on Earth, you also want to look at eliminating bad debt and creating good debt.

Bad debt is any debt incurred from consumption, including credit card, car loans, mortgage and student loans.

Good debt is where you borrow money to make money on an investment. This can include start-up money for a business, mortgage for property with a rental income greater than the mortgage, or other investments. So only borrow money for investment, not consumption.

Your ability to discipline yourself in working toward a goal is a testament of your character where you successfully control your spending urges. If your spending was out of control and you have created bad debt then you need to eliminate it.

How to Eliminate Credit Card Debt:

1. Pay off the debt with the highest interest rate first because it is costing you the most money.
2. With credit card debt pay off the card with the lowest balance first. Say for example you have cards with $1000, $5000 and $8000 balances. You first pay the $1000 off along with making the minimum payment on each card, then move to the next balance until all your cards are paid.
3. Take money out of your savings account, and use it to pay off your credit card debt, since the interest charged on your credit card debt costs you more than what you earn from a savings account.
4. Continue the process until all your debts are paid off

If your debt is unmanageable and you need a new start, consider debt consolidation and bankruptcy options with a trustee. Once your debt is under control, you want to establish good credit history as indicated by your FICO Credit score used by creditors to decide whether to lend money to you and at what rate. Basically the FICO score rewards disciplined habits:

1. Make monthly payments on-time with credit cards and bills
2. Pay your balances in full each month. Use credit card for convenience, not to charge money that you do not have.
3. Check your credit report for mistakes and irregularities

With a strong FICO score 760 or more, you easily qualify for loans and get the best rates. You can get access to loans, grants, aid and even housing, simply based on your credit reputation. Your payment history makes up 35% of your FICO score and your debt to credit ratio is 30%. Both together make up 65% of your score and are the two biggest factors in your credit score.

Realize that your spending habits are being reported and evaluated by lenders. Your wise spending habits can allow you to built a solid financial reputation and also create the habits that will help you to grow financially in future.

Self-Awareness is the Key

Decisions at Earth are based on self-awareness as to whether they are decisions about your finances, relationships or growth. Exercise awareness of your goals. Consider your reason for investing. Are you looking for a tax shelter? Are you saving money for a home with rental income? Are you saving to eliminate debt, or to pay for a purchase such as a car or a vacation?

Character is the First Step to Prosperity

As with other key areas of life, your character begins your journey to wealth. Sometimes due to anxiety and fear you can develop a contracted relationship with money where your trust in the Universe is lost. The only way you can overcome these emotions is to voice them.

For you, the fear might have an image: Becoming a bag lady or a homeless old man, losing your job, or home. Explore the fear and then use it to motivate you in your goal for greater financial freedom, including eliminating bad debt, saving money and considering the right investment for your goals.

You need to also be gentle and compassionate with yourself and others. If you lack money or know someone who does, it is never indicative of God's punishment.

Also, it is not necessarily the person's lack of desire or intelligence. Mostly, poverty stems from lack of external supports: Cash, opportunity, family support, or financial knowledge.

You can with patience overcome these things and your ability to rise above them will form your character qualities of patience, steadfastness and discipline, which are also the qualities needed to nurture and keep wealth.

Money acquired through self-development is more likely to stay with you, than if you received it through a lottery, inheritance, illegal or dishonest means. Besides external obstacles, Suze Orman in *Courage to Be Rich* describes emotional obstacles to wealth. They include:

	Description	*Expression*
Shame	When you believe that you are not good enough to deserve financial success.	Self-defeating and sabotage behaviours.
Fear	Grasping tendencies with money where relinquishing your hold on it is difficult	Constant worry that interrupts sleep and keeps you from enjoying life
Anger	Keeps you from welcoming money and people.	Clenched fist, mouth and forehead.

Shame arises when you are disconnected from cleansing energies of the Water center. It is released by Self-acceptance when you know that you did your best and that you have learned from the experience. So wash away the dirt of shame in the waters of forgiveness. Fearful thoughts arise from aspects of the Air center, and through positive thinking you develop Self-confidence. Then you are able to overcome fear. As you trust yourself and the Universe to provide, your fears start to dissipate.

When you lose connection to the warmth and purification of Fire, then Anger can reside in your heart. You heal the anger through Self-transcendence by which your vision is enlarged. You soon realize that the anger is hurting you and through forgiveness of anyone who may have hurt you, only then can your heart heal.

Earth Symbols

Square

The geometric symbol of Earth is shown in the square, cube or rectangle, since Earth contains, while Spirit expands. The square is a secure shape, so it is used in rooms and houses.

Pentagram

The primary symbol of Wicca and used in esoteric European magic. The five points of the Star represent the five elements. The outer circle binds the elements together, which is representative of Earthly or natural energies and contains all the elements.

The Sun Cross

A circle filled with a cross points to the four elements at the points and the fifth element Spirit is at the centre. The four points also represent the four directions on Earth: North, South, East, West.

The Cross

The Cross is a symbol of Christianity, representing the Sacrifice and Resurrection of Jesus. So it became the symbol of eternal life and triumph over death. The Incarnation represents Spirit coming to Earth. In non-Christian traditions, the cross has depicted the world-axis with horizontal representing Earth and vertical the Spirit.

The Cosmic Dance of Shiva

Shiva's Cosmic Dance depicted in statues symbolizes the cosmic cycles of creation and destruction, and the daily cycle of birth and death on Earth.

Authentic Wealth

Authentic Wealth emerges from your core values in alignment with all the Five Elements, bringing Spiritual, Psychological, Relational, Intuitional and Physical aspects of life into Total Wealth and Well-being. This is a complete accounting system, where money has an honoured place, yet it is in service of your life and goals, not an end in itself. You serve Spirit first, then people, then money and lastly things. Through relationships you establish financial goals and decisions because money is in service of Spirit, yourself and others.

Wisdom in your spending habits with fiscal responsibility in mind will determine the opportunities you can afford for yourself and your loved ones. The money you can save and nurture will serve you better than things that you acquire, which often just add to clutter in your home. So before you buy an idea, really think whether you really need, want or value purchasing it.

Character development involves the ability to delay gratification and to live within your means, while also working toward a lasting goal of increasing your means. So many items that you want are just things of little long-term value. Multiplication of wants and material possessions is less important than the purification of your durable character qualities, including Confidence, Love, Integrity, Responsibility and Awareness.

Even after you have successfully increased your financial means, you still have a responsibility to ethically use your money to make the world a better place through sharing some of your wealth with others or to give to a good cause.

You also need to balance financial growth with abundance in all areas of your life, including growth in relationships, health, spiritual life, mind and with a compassionate heart.

You also want to look after the environment which ultimately creates your real abundance because all life depends upon clean air, clean water and healthy soil.

Regardless of where you are at now, you can always feel uplifted by people, pets, music and art. Nature is one of the best places to feel enriched.

Plants and Nature

One of the best ways to commune with Earth energies is to go for a walk in nature, noticing the trees, plants, animals and weather. Another activity that grounds you to Earth is spending time in your garden or through gardening. As you open yourself to the beauty and vitality of nature, your Spirit will feel uplifted and inspired. When in nature practice these suggestions:

- Let go of all intentions and be in the present moment
- Fully participate with all your senses in the experience
- Spend at least 15 minutes a day outside

You can also bring the outside earth energies indoors through plants, rocks, wood, seashells and other natural objects. Plants also improve indoor air quality. Maintain the plants in good health as the growth of plants symbolizes your own growth.

Welcome Earth into Your Space

Bring energies of the earth through symbols into your kitchen such as a bowl of fresh fruit or lemons, a vase with fresh flowers, and a living plant. The kitchen represents Motherly nurturing energies, prosperity and well-being. Consider the importance of healthy, fresh foods for maintaining your well-being.

The Recreation Room in your home can be empty or filled with symbols of personal meaning to you. Either way this space is connected to your body, which represents all that is physical, earthly and of good health. As part of your overall well-being, consider the importance of exercise in your life.

Incorporate physical fitness into your life, where you can combine strength training, aerobics and stretching exercises to increase and maintain your health.

The following exercise will further your connection to Earth:

Earth Centre Visualization

1. Imagine a beam of light descending from the Water navel centre through your hips, legs and then collecting at your feet.
2. There it forms a green pulsating sphere of light
3. Vibrate/affirm 'I Bless' four times and realize your presence on Earth blesses all who come in contact with you.
4. Spend some time and boost the Earth energy here.
5. Now imagine five orbs of wealth forming a central pillar in your body:
   a. **Spiritual Wealth**: Golden orb of Spirit at the Crown
      Affirm: 'I Am' and envision: The Heavens
   b. **Psychological Wealth**: Violet orb of Air at the Throat
      Affirm: 'I Think' and envision: The Sky
   c. **Relational Wealth**: Red sphere of Fire at your Heart
      Affirm: 'I Love' and envision: The Sun/Stars
   d. **Intuitive Wealth**: Blue sphere of Water at your Navel
      Affirm: 'I Will' and envision: The Ocean/Moon
   e. **Physical Wealth**: Green circle of Earth at your Feet
      Affirm: 'I Bless' and envision: The Earth as a globe viewed from outer space without any divisions or boundaries.
6. Allow this image or sense of the Energy centres to become vivid as you move your attention successively from one centre to the next. Practice this meditative visualization whenever you wish to activate your energy centres. Remember that this is a suggested practice. If you prefer create your own practice by using this book as a resource tool

to discover a variety of ways to *activate the five elements*, which will lead to the manifestation of greater abundance and total wealth in your life.

The Fruits of the Mature Tree

You have journeyed from planting the potential of abundant life in Spirit, to seeding belief at Air in your thought, then creating expansion of that seed into a sapling through the warmth of Fire.

Next, you watered the sapling for increased growth both on the surface and under the roots as conscious and subconscious energies were united. Finally, with Earth you realized the Fruits of your development as a fully mature human being who can manifest total wealth in all areas of life.

You have activated each energy centre from Spirit, to Air, Fire, Water, and then finally Earth.

Bibliography for Chapter 9

Anielski, Mark.   *The Economics of Happiness.*

Bradler & Schneider.   *Feng Shui Symbols.*

Cirlot, J.E.   *A Dictionary of Symbols.*

Khalfani, Lynette.   *The Money Coach's Guide.*
                       To Your First Million.

Kiyosaki, Robert T.   *Rich Dad's Cashflow Quadrant.*

Orman, Suze.   *Courage to be Rich.*
                       The 9 Steps to Financial Freedom.
                       Women & Money.

Trump, Donald &   *Why We Want You to Be Rich.*
Robert Kiyosaki.

Tyson, Eric & Tony   *Personal Finance for Canadians for*
Martin.   *Dummies.*

Whitehurst, Ellen.   *Make this Your Lucky Day.*

Circulating the Energy:
A Final Exercise for the Five Energy Centres

This exercise is based on *The Art of True Healing* by Israel Regardie, allowing the circulation of energy. Here is the exercise:

1. Imagine great energy circulating rapidly at the crown of your head. This great spiritual energy is available for any activity in daily life, offering joy, peace and unity.
2. Imagine the energy flowing down like a stream down the left side of the head, face, trunk, hips and the leg. While the current is descending, slowly exhale the breath.
3. Then slowly inhale, then imagine or visualize the stream passes from the left foot to the right foot, and gradually rises on the right side of the body, going up the leg, hips, trunk, face and the crown.
4. The energy returns to the crown, the contact-point of Spirit, from where it issued. This creates a closed *Circuit One* of vital energy.
5. Now imagine as you exhale the energy flowing within the body from the front.
6. It touches the Energy centres of Air at the throat, Fire at the heart, Water at the navel, and the feet where Earth energy resides.
7. The energy goes from the front of the feet to the back and as you inhale the energy goes back up through Earth, Water, Fire, Air and returns to Spirit. This is *Circuit Two*.
8. Practice circulating the energy a few more times and let it return to the Spirit Centre at the crown.
9. Now circulate the energy again but this time look for a centre that needs balance or to be further activated. Spend more time at this centre and bring it into alignment by sending the flow of energy there.
10. Then let the energy circulate, forming a circuit on the outside and centre of the body. Imagine Circuit One and Circuit Two rapidly moving and energizing your whole body and all the Elemental Centres in unison.

Chapter **10**

You Have Arrived

Change begins within
Paul McCartney/Ringo Starr

Most of the leaders in the past missed the great part of The Secret, which is to empower and share with others
Dr. Dennis Waitley

The heart that gives, gathers
Marianne Moore

Throw your heart over the fence and the rest will follow
Norman Vincent Peale

A BRIDGE TOWARD DEEPER UNDERSTANDING

With our book *The Law of Attraction: Making it Work for You* we have created a *bridge* for you toward deeper understanding about how to transform your life to achieve happiness and contentment that goes beyond amassing merely financial wealth alone. As you journey across the *bridge* you will delve deeply into spiritual and enlightening insights so that you will clearly know how to utilize the Law of Attraction to manifest success and abundance in your life- not just financially but on many different levels.

As you have seen, there is more to the Law of Attraction than just wishful thinking. Furthermore, there is ample room with the Law of Attraction for sincerity, compassion and generosity toward others. We are all in this together! With an inspired and co-operative spirit we can truly create a world that works for everyone. Clearly, blame of self or others for experiencing life challenges is counter-productive to manifesting abundance!

With an open mind and faith, let Universal life energy flow through you for growth and healing of all aspects of life experience for yourself and others. Whether you are faced with joyful or sorrowful life situations, maintain an attitude of gratitude and never give up!

Take a second look at the cover of our book. If you look very carefully at the sun you will notice that you cannot distinguish whether this is a picture of a sunrise or a sunset. How true to life, and, as Rose Dean (sister of Deborah) so eloquently points out 'Sunrise or Sunset? It's all in your attitude!' Approach life with this open- minded perspective and you will activate energy flow along with the experience of transformation and abundance.

Be open and grateful for the light that is manifest now. Know that right now, at this point in history as never before, we are standing on new ground, living on a New Earth, in a time of miracle energy where it is possible to experience awesome life enrichment.

Know that ultimately it does not matter what happens since your personal response to life events is of utmost importance; and know that whatever happens will be best for your soul!

From a Universal perspective everything happens for the highest good! All is Well! When a door seems closed before you there is no need for worry. As you work with the Law of Attraction know that sooner or later a greater opportunity will manifest. Be aware that if a closed door had opened it might have prevented a new opportunity from presenting itself.

Be filled with serenity and inner peace as you await a new opening in your life, with new possibilities. Have the wisdom and patience to let time do its work in your life and affairs. Welcome every step with serenity. It's all in your attitude and perspective!

Inner peace is a source of Infinite Love and Light for you. To rejuvenate remember to consciously connect with your inner source of peace and not from external sources. Your power is always within!

Know that as you attune to Divine Universal Love and let it flow through every cell of your being you will begin to realize your full potential.

Finally, let go of fears and align yourself with Faith and Trust in the Universe and with your Inner Peace. Know that in your Centre you always have access to Spirit. Discover what is true for you. Be authentic and express more of who you really are. Dare to be yourself! In creating a bridge toward deeper understanding of the Law of Attraction we have provided you with practical ways to attain positive, progressive life transformations. We've also expanded on the definition of what true prosperity is along with delving into what various world religions/spiritual paths provide about insight into Total Wealth.

We have also offered extensive wisdom about symbols and how you may use them to empower your Law of Attraction practice.

Finally, we have taken you on a fascinating journey through the Five Elements and your inner Energy Centres, providing you with tools to activate the manifestation of prosperity in your life.

Work with our *life suggestions* of meditations, exercises and approaches, as you feel inspired to do so. Do what works for you and feels right for you. Be authentic and be yourself! Be creative! With our approach you may easily work on manifesting abundance in your life by connecting with *Spirit*, clarifying your intention by means of your positive thought and as you *Believe.*

Then, *Activate* your Energy Centres by creatively working with the Five Elements, Angels and Symbols as you are inspired to do so. Finally, *Receive* whatever manifests with an open heart and mind, maintaining a state of serenity and inner peace as you continue with optimism, faith and trust in the Universe.

Now you are ready to repeat the process from the beginning once again in order to manifest your next heart's desire.

Approach your Law of Attraction practice with mindfulness. Realistically, you cannot judge yourself or another at any point along the way- after all you never really know if a particular life experience ultimately plays out as a *sunrise* or a *sunset.* Besides, *judgment* de-energizes your being, constricts the flow of Universal energy and synchronicity!

So then, what's most important is to remain a conscious co-creator with the Universe in order to energize and enliven your life and the lives of others; while maintaining a spirit of doing, to the best of your understanding, what is for the highest good of one and all.

A NEW ERA OF UNIVERSAL WELLNESS

Remember that the Law of Attraction is really all about *perspective* and *attitude!*

Therefore, see your world as lifting out of mere survival and chaos, into a new era of Universal wellness, peace, and infinite possibility. In order to do this it is most important to acknowledge and appreciate all that you have right now, along with actively giving back to others. Amplify your vision of True Wealth and extend the benefits of prosperity for yourself and others in order to move beyond survival and into Wholeness.

With this approach you will experience accelerated results. Know that you have the power to access inner greatness, healthy living and radiant wealth.

SEE YOUR LIFE AS BLESSED AND EMPOWERED

Remember to activate your Will and direct your attention to the Highest within your Heart, and know that as inspiration from the Divine. If you see your life as blessed and empowered then this attitude enhances your state of well-being and the flow of synchronistic Universal Energy in your life.

Send this awareness of well-being out to the World as a peaceful knowing trust that solutions to Humanity's greatest challenges as well as those of your own exist within, and are ready to be brought forward by your ever-present, inherent power of co-creation with the Universe.

BE CREATORS OF WEALTH AND VALUE

Intend wealth, peace and sustainable prosperity for yourself, everyone you know and for your global family. Be creators of Wealth, Value and Virtue in order to activate the momentum/synergy of total personal prosperity, along with Global Wealth.

By maintaining an open mind along with a state of equanimity you will accelerate the *attraction* of unlimited possibilities for growth and sustainable wealth creation.

We suggest that to further empower this process consciously *attract* and share wealth not only at a personal level but also at a global level.

Here is our Wealth Activation Formula:

Spirit
Believe
Activate
Receive

You have the freedom to create that vision and opportunity for yourself and give that vision and opportunity to others.

YOU MAKE THE DECISION

You and only you can make the decision to live in your *highest integrity*! By living in your *highest integrity* you can create wealth along with a lifestyle of service to humanity.

Envision yourself as a wealthy individual and by this we mean *Total Wealth*. See yourself as a person who is able to connect to others whose intention is to unlock *Peace* and *Prosperity*, freedom and financial power that is good not only for yourself but for the entire world as well.

We are advocating a *Spiritual* and *Heart-Based* wealth attraction approach for anyone and everyone who desires to see themselves as powerful co-creators. This is for you!

Be certain to share this Law of Attraction wisdom with others, as well as put it into practice for yourself. Intend to see and attract resources for freedom, prosperity, well-being and healthy sustainable living for one and all. *You make the decision!*

With this in mind, we suggest that you consciously consider the Law of Attraction philosophical and practical approaches that we have provided in this book. Integrate into your life that which is comfortable and rings true for you. Set the rest aside to perhaps use at a later time if you feel so inclined.

In order to activate your Energy centres and the balanced flow of the five elements in your life, experiment with our suggested life approaches or create your own; whatever you are intuitively guided to do.

Develop a unique approach for yourself that is custom made and inspirational. Maintain realistic expectations and remember to *expect the unexpected.* Be true to yourself and express more of who you really are.

Practice prosperity wisdom with an open mind, creativity, inspiration and an over-flowing heart.

It is our sincere wish that the Universe be abundantly generous with you, so that you may manifest your dreams and so that you may also be abundantly generous with others.

Remember that infinite possibilities are born of Faith in: Spirit, Universal timing, yourself and others. May you feel the presence of *Inner Peace*; you have arrived!

About the Authors

Both authors co-wrote bestseller novel **NEXUS**, now in its 4th printing, after having received numerous rave reviews and having also been paired with **The Secret** and **The Law of Attraction** books by amazon.com and other major online retailers.

 **Deborah Morrison** is a poet, author and speaker from Hamilton, Ontario, who is moved by the healing power of the written word, nature and people. As a psychotherapist/counsellor, early childhood educator, and yoga instructor, she has used her abilities to foster growth and learning. She holds an Honours Degree in Religious Studies/Sociology from McMaster University and has undergone extensive research in Eastern and Western thought within the framework of contemporary and comparative studies. She has written several published articles on natural therapies, yoga, psychology and metaphysics. She is a distinguished member of the International Society of Poetry and has had numerous poems published through the International Library of Poetry. She also wrote the inspirational book *Mystical Poetry.*

 **Arvind Singh** is a thoughtful, spiritual and creative individual, who asks the big questions in life. Why are we here? How do you live a good life? What is real and what is unreal? He holds an Honours B.A. in History from McMaster University. He has researched spirituality and religion from a multi-disciplinary perspective with the rare ability to highlight the essence of compassion and truth. With an interest in different cultures and growing up in Canada which welcomes diversity, he has found many eclectic sources of wisdom. He has written several published magazine and newspaper articles in both English and South Asian languages. He enjoys taking the reader on a journey through words with spiritual depth, understanding and inspiration.

Manor House
905-648-2193
www.manor-house.biz